JOHN WALKER'S COMMONPLACE BOOK

John Walker's Commonplace Book

A TRAVELLER IN THE 1670s

EDITED BY

Anthea Jones

THE HOBNOB PRESS

First published in the United Kingdom in 2025

by The Hobnob Press,
8 Lock Warehouse, Severn Road, Gloucester GL1 2GA
www.hobnobpress.co.uk

British Library Cataloguing in Publication Data
A catalogue record for this book is available from the British Library

ISBN 978-1-914407-86-4

Typeset in Adobe Garamond Pro 11/14 pt.
Typesetting and origination by John Chandler

Cover illustration: 'The Pont du Gard, near Nimes', drawn by T. Allom and engraved by A. Willmore, c.1841, with later hand colouring.

CONTENTS

ACKNOWLEDGEMENTS

The contribution made by the publisher of *John Walker's Commonplace Book* has been much greater than any editor has the right to expect, and is warmly acknowledged. It has been difficult to make the transcript of Walker's manuscript as faithful as possible while modernising some particular aspects of Walker's script so as to make the text as accessible as possible to a twenty-first century reader. John Chandler of Hobnob Press has amended uncomplainingly where the editor has been at fault in the first, and indeed in the second draft, and has made the final text much more consistent than the initial transcript.

Further, John Chandler is thanked for preparing the maps which display Walker's routes, adding considerably to the impact and clarity of the accounts of his journeys. At the same time, yet another valuable contribution which John Chandler has made to *John Walker's Commonplace Book* is to translate the Latin epitaphs and inscriptions which Walker copied down, and they are in the Appendix, referenced by page number.

Archivists of Somersetshire Heritage Centre scanned Walker's accounts of his ten journeys in the Commonplace Book, and they are thanked for their willing and pleasant help in providing copy for the transcription.

There will be errors, particularly in identifying places mentioned in the text, and the editor apologises for these which are entirely her responsibility. It is hoped that the final text provides many readers with interest and also insights into seventeenth century conditions not only in England, Scotland and Wales, but also in the Channel Islands, the Low Countries and France.

PREFACE

John Walker's Commonplace Book is the second Hobnob Press publication which makes available accounts of journeys made in the later seventeenth century by a leisured English gentleman. John Walker stated precisely the dates when he was travelling round the country; *Thomas Baskerville: Journeys in Industrious England* was less precise, but the accounts were written up in the 1680s from notes kept during his travels, which therefore took place probably in the 1670s. A decade after the restoration of Charles II, there was relative peace in the country, though both Walker and Baskerville commented on the destruction of the civil war still to be seen.

Transcribing the writings of Thomas Baskerville suggested to the editor that it would be interesting to compare his accounts of England with another writer's. But were there any, close in date, available for the comparison? Celia Fiennes was travelling a little later in the century. Looking through *The Observant Traveller*, a compilation of unpublished sources in Archives Offices listed in 1989, it seemed there were few to choose from, but the *Commonplace Book* of John Walker was very close in date and his journeys covered areas of England described by Baskerville.

Comparisons between the accounts reveal two rather different views of England in the 1670s. Both men visited what were clearly the principal targets of sightseers, then as they are today: cathedrals, and the county towns, partly because they were large enough to provide good accommodation for the traveller and for the Assize judges; both noted when there were Assizes at the time of their visits. Walker was not inclined to say more than that accommodation was adequate or in many cases inadequate. Baskerville was more expansive, describing the actual dishes served to him and his man, and commenting on the availability of wine and beer. Even in his six months tour of France, Walker did not comment on food and very rarely on wine.

Both men took a keen interest in the state of the economy. Walker generally took the view that the government could do much more to encourage trade; Baskerville on the other hand noted a considerable amount of small-scale industrial activity. This reflects to a large extent Walker's attitude to the restored Stuart monarchy. He was clearly not a devoted royalist. He was also to some extent a politician, the son of a man deeply involved in the split between royalists and parliamentarians, Puritans and Presbyterians. He occasionally made sarcastic comments on the restoration. Though he regarded himself as a country gentleman, Walker lived in London, and was associated with those involved in the court. Baskerville was more purely a countryman.

Walker was a more adventurous traveller than Baskerville, touring round Wales and reaching as far as Edinburgh and Glasgow in Scotland. He was willing to undertake sea voyages; Baskerville had experienced them as a very young man and had perhaps had enough of sea travel by the time he was journeying in England. In his travels both in England and abroad, Walker had a critical outlook on the political situations he encountered, and amongst his very interesting comments are comparisons between legal practices in England and France. He saw that war on the continent was a constant pre-occupation, and the tendency to aggrandisement of the French king caused smaller and more vulnerable countries to spend time and money on fortifying their towns. He noted the great wealth of Louis XIV without much critical comment, but was clearly impressed with the ambitious water works in the royal gardens he visited.

Both books have many points of comparison and naturally also differences relating to social position and to character. *John Walker's Commonplace Book* offers many insights into scenes and political situations, and ranges more widely than Thomas Baskerville's *Journeys*. It is pleasing to find Hobnob Press adding this volume to their growing collection of traveller's tales.

Anthea Jones
24 February 2025

INTRODUCTION

'Having spent some weekes in Northamptonshire, least sloth, and laziness the contagion of cuntry-gentlemen should prevaile upon mee I determin'd to traverse some parts of the adjacent counties. With this resolution on the 3d of 7br. this yeare I sett forward'.

John Walker's admonition to himself, written in 1678, followed an account of journeys he had made in each of the preceeding seven years: across England, through Wales, into Scotland, to the Channel Islands, and to the Low Countries and France. Sloth was not apparently his master. His description of himself as a country gentleman, however, is revealing. In his will he names 'all and every my Lands Tenements and Hereditaments scituate lying and being in the townshipps of High Barnett alias Chipping Barnett South Mymms Hadley and Ridge and elsewhere in the counties of Middlesex and Hertfordshire'.[1] There is no mention of Northamptonshire, but he was possibly staying with family or friends; the previous year he had spent time at Findon or Thingdon.[2] Hadley, or Monken Hadley, in Middlesex, in the corner of Enfield Chase, was at a later date his country residence; after his death his wife described herself as of Monken Hadley, and wished to be decently buried there.[3] It was a wealthy hill-top area by 1664, when 8 houses had ten or more hearths. However, in his will made in 1692, at the time he was getting married to Cecil Heneage, John Walker gave his principal

---

1 TNA/Prob11/476/112. It is possible that the Walker family had possessed land in South Mimms in the sixteenth century. *British History Online* https://www.british-history.ac.uk/vch/middx/vol5/pp282-285 [accessed 31 December 2024]

2 Findon (occasionally Finedon), alternatively known as Thingdon (Lewis's *Topographical Dictionary*), the older form of the name. Walker possibly had property here. There was a Walker charity for a boy's free school recorded in the National Gazetteer of Great Britain and Ireland (1868).

3 *VCH Mddx* vol 5; notable inhabitants in the seventeenth century included Sir Robert Atkyns the Gloucestershire historian. Monken Hadley was convenient for Londoners, lying along the Great North Road. Somerset Heritage Centre (SHC)/ DD/WHb/70; 74.

residence as the Inner Temple, London. He gave himself the title of Esquire.[4]

Chief Usher of the Court of Exchequer

JOHN WALKER ALSO had a source of income and considerable status, which he described in his will as 'my office and offices of Cheife Usher of the Court of Exchequer and Marshall Proclamator and Barrier of the Court of Common Pleas and Justices in Eyre with all houses rights members ffees advantages hereditaments and appurtenances whatsoever therunto belonging or in anywise appertaining'. He did not discharge these duties in person but appointed deputies, profiting nonetheless from the numerous fees and perquisites.

This hereditary office was held in fee under the terms of a grant made about 1156 by Henry II; it was not abolished until 1842.[5] John Walker's grandfather, Thomas Walker, described as of Westminster, esquire, had purchased the office in 1603 from William Maddocks or Maddox for £1475 and took possession in 1613; he also married William Maddocks' widow. Thomas was the first Walker to hold the office.[6]

Amongst copies of documents written at the reverse end of the Commonplace book is a summary statement of the duties of the office from which it appears that the holder took an oath of admission to the Office: 'That the office of Chiefe Usher of the Court of Exchequor (with the appertenants) is a very ancient inheritance held by Grand Serjeanty from the Crowne as may appeare by severall Records of the sayd Court.

That the duty of the Officer is to look after the sd Court and the respective offices thereunto belonging (as much as in him lyes) as may appeare by the oath which he takes att his admission into the sayd Office.'

A fuller account of the office was compiled in 1642. 'The Cheife Usher hath the Custody of the Court Exchequer Chamber, & house with all the appurtenances and hath the generall keeping of all the Records there and waites upon the Lord Treasurer & Chauncellor when they come thither, & serves the Court & all the officers, with all kind of necessaries as paper Incke, Standishes, Statute bookes &c. for which he hath his liberte each Terme for the allowance & payment thereof signed by the Chauncellor of the Exchequer'.[7]

4　There is a draft copy of his will in SHC/DD/WHb/66, apparently drafted as he married Cecil Heneage, also of the will as proved in 1704, DD/WHb/60.

5　Parliamentary Archives: GB-061/ECU.

6　SHC/account of Button, Walker and Heneage families, making use of extensive family pedigrees. The date of Thomas Walker's purchase appears to be 1603. DD/WHb/136. Parliamentary Archives: GB-061/ECU.

7　Parliamentary Archives: GB-061/ECU.

From Thomas Walker the office passed to his son Clement, who in 1634 when he married his second wife, Mary Button, the daughter and heiress of Sir William Button 1st baronet, endowed her with the office as her jointure.[8] It appears from other documents copied in the reverse end of the Commonplace book, however, that enjoyment of this undoubtedly lucrative office was not straightforward. There were clearly problems with the inheritance for John, Clement's youngest son, and his mother Mary, in which Clement's son William by his first wife was involved. Mary eventually prevailed, and she was able to pass the office to her son John in 1662, 'the mediate Remainder whereof being to the said John Walker and his heirs for ever'.[9] The deed may indicate that John had reached 21 years of age, and if so was born in 1641.

Other copies of legal documents in the Commonplace Book indicate a dispute over the use of the house in Palace Yard. The papers are not dated, but one of the Walkers refused to allow his house to be used to entertain the Danish ambassadors and their retinue, and was imprisoned for contempt and deprived of his office. It appears that this may have been one more example of the king of the time, probably Charles I, trying to recover some valuable estate lost to the Crown. The document records a legal opinion that the commitment was not legal. Walker seems to have won this case.

Clement Walker and John Walker

CLEMENT WALKER'S MARRIAGE with Mary Button, and John Walker's with Cecil Heneage, brought the Walkers into alliance with important Somerset landowners. Clement laid the foundations when he acquired the estate of Charterhouse or Charterhouse-on-Mendip, an extra-parochial area in Somerset, now in the parish of Priddy. He took some part in Somerset affairs during the civil war; he had also been elected MP for Wells during the Long Parliament. He was a scholar and a noted legal authority on the English parliament; while he was a moderate supporter of parliament's arguments with Charles I, he wished to make an accommodation with the king, and criticised the extreme views of both presbyterians and puritans. His reputation was somewhat sullied by the apparently widely-known fact, despite the wish of her father to cover up the event, that he had attempted to stab his wife.[10] The lady recovered and the marriage continued for a few more years, but she died a few years later, enabling Clement to marry his second wife. From that time, the office of Chief Usher stayed in the Walker and Heneage families for generations.

---

8   ODNB. Retrieved 1 Jan. 2025, from https://www.oxforddnb.com/view/10.
9   SHC/DD/WHb/147.
10   ODNB.

If he was born in 1641, John Walker was too young to have much knowledge or experience of the civil wars, and his father died in 1651 while imprisoned in the Tower for his outspoken views and the many pamphlets he published critical of Oliver Cromwell and the capture of parliament by radical nonconformists.[11] His youngest son seems to have absorbed his father's strong prejudice against Roman Catholics. While he was probably ten years old when his father died, he seems also to have accquired a keen interest in politics; a number of the pages at the reverse end of the Commonplace book are concerned with parliament's arguments with Charles II in 1673 over the intended marriage of his brother James with the 14-year old Mary of Modena, a strong adherent of the Roman Catholic church. At the same time, surrounded by lawyers and aristocratic politicians as Chief Usher of the Exchequer, Walker was immersed in the politics of the period. He had probably acquired from his father (and possibly his mother too) a moderately royalist viewpoint at the same time as being a strong supporter of the rights of parliament. He thought it important to record at the back of the Commonplace book the certificate of his taking Holy Communion in 1673, so demonstrating that he was not a Roman Catholic nor a nonconformist.

Anthony á Wood recorded that Clement's son, John, had informed him that his father had studied at Christ Church, Oxford, and also informed him of the date of his father's death. á Wood mentioned that John was a gentleman commoner of Lincoln College and his matriculation is recorded in 1658, when he would have been about 17 years of page. Yet from the way in which John Walker describes his journey to Oxford, on his way to Wales, it seems that he probably spent little time in the university. Between 1658 and his visit to the colleges in 1676, he noted with strong disapprobation the 'many superstitious Roman ceremonies to bee yet retained in their chappels'.

The main outline of John Walker's life has been established from the archives preserved by the Heneage family, though these are all of a legal nature; his character remains largely obscure. In his accounts of his journeys he gives little information about himself. In the 1670s he was presumably in his 30s, young enough to endure the sometimes hazardous and uncomfortable conditions of his travels, and to be willing to crawl through tunnels and lie flat on the gound to hear stones falling in Eldon Hole in the Peak district.[12]

Walker probably always travelled with a man. In his will he bequeathed

11   Anthony á Wood, ed. Philip Bliss 1813-20, *Athenae Oxoniensis vol 3, 291-5*.

12   Disembarking from a channel crossing remained hazardous in the following century. Jeremy Black, *The Grand Tour in the Eighteenth Century (1992 reprinted Sandpiper Books 1999), 17.*

£500 to Richard Crew, his servant, suggesting considerable respect and that his servant had been in his service for some years.[13] He refers to the cost of taking a coach or transport by boat for himself and his man, but rarely gives any hint of the closeness of the relationship, never mentioning his man's comments on the journeys, or on the sights seen. Once in Scotland, in a poor village, he rather dramatically records that 'the verry rats were like to eat up my Companions coat for hunger', the only occasion he uses this more familiar description. Companionship must have existed during the six months of the second visit to France, and his companion must have been as good a horseman as Walker. There are few accounts of any mishaps.

When he was over 50 years of age, in 1692, John Walker, then of Hadley in Middlesex, married Cecil Heneage, daughter and heiress of Sir Michael Heneage. He wrote his will at that time, putting his wife in possession of the office of Chief Usher. Subsequently the couple had two sons, the elder also named John, but his father died in 1704, so that as with John Walker senr, John Walker jnr's upbringing was largely the responsibility of his mother Cecil. In 1714, Cecil bound her son aprentice to Justis Beck of London, merchant. The apprenticeship was to last for six years.[14] It suggests John jnr was born about 1697. A number of documents in the archive relate to John jnr. John and Cecil Walker had a second son, Heneage Walker, to whom she bequeathed her books and goods at Hadley. John jnr was her executor.[15]

The Commonplace book

THE INVENTION OF paper unlocked the possibility of the Commonplace book or notebook, consisting of small sheets of paper bound together in which miscellaneous items of interest could be recorded. Such paper books were becoming common in the Italian states in the thirteenth century, especially in Florence and Genoa. There are some famous notebooks from the late fifteenth century, particularly those of Leonardo da Vinci. Geoffrey Chaucer knew of them: Jankyn, the husband of the Wife of Bath, taunted his wife with reading extracts in a notebook concerning wicked wives.[16] Chaucer had been a diplomat and negotiator, travelling to Florence where he may have been able to appreciate the value of the commonplace books, but not many English examples survive from this period. By the seventeenth century notebooks became widely used in Europe. The diaries of Samuel Pepys which

---

13 TNA/Prob11/476/112.
14 SHC/DD/WHb/70.
15 SHC/DD/WHb/74.
16 Roland Allen, *The Notebook A History of Thinking on Paper (2023)*, 88-93.

he wrote between 1660 and 1669 are a well-known example though not published until the nineteenth century.

John Walker's notebook is bound in white leather. It is quite a small book, 160mm x 104mm x 17mm approx. There appear to be 9 gatherings of 32pp sections fastened with three cords. The book is one item in the large deposit of archives in Somerset Heritage Centre, accepted in lieu of Inheritance Tax by H M Government and allocated to the Somerset Heritage Centre, 2015, with additional contributions, and called the *Button-Walker-Heneage Muniments*; successive intermarriages combine to make up the family pedigree of these three families, which members had extensively researched.

At the beginning of the commonplace book Walker seems to have set out to record some political material which he regarded as significant. First there is an 'Affidavit concerning the fiering of ye Citty of London in July Anno 1670', by Thomas Rowe, of Barnard's Inn, gent., which implied that it might have been linked with a Popish plot; such was the fevered atmosphere of the period. A second document was a speech made [or to be made] in the House of Lords complaining of a Bill sent up by the Commons 'for giveing vnto his Majesty the 20th part of our real estates', etc. which is undated. Thirdly Walker copied out King James's 'peremptory letter to the Lower House of Parliament', also undated. The last item before the accounts of his travels was 'The Earl of Clare's Speech in the House of Lords' 21 Feb. 1670/1. These items it may be presumed were all written by John Walker, since his father had died some twenty years before, unless they had been written by another relative or acquaintance and the book subsequently passed to him.

In particular the peremptory letter from James II does chime with Walker's strong prejudice against the Roman Catholic church as shown frequently in his travel writing, and his fear, shared by many in the House of Commons, that James would attempt officially to reintroduce Roman Catholicism to England. The fear was greatly stimulated by James's choice of a bride. These four documents were followed by the closely-written pages of accounts of his ten journeys both in Great Britain and across the sea, a transcript of which is published here.

Not many such accounts of travels in the seventeenth century have been published, in contrast with the following century when many gentlemen travelled abroad for their education as well as for pleasure and wrote about their experiences; some wrote intending their accounts to be published.[17] Esther Moir, in a list of both published and manuscript sources relating to travel in Great Britain, found a rather small number of seventeenth century or

17 Black, *The Grand Tour, Introduction.*

earlier sources, and her list included the notes of John Leland which circulated amongst accademics and friends, but were not published for hundreds of years; the list also included the extensive writings of John Taylor the 'water poet', who published his own writings.[18] The restoration of the monarchy in 1660 brought back to Great Britain numbers of royalist sympathisers who had spent time abroad during the civil war period, who no doubt encouraged their families to take an interest in the ways of countries across the Channel. The restoration also brought someone like William Schellink, a Dutchman, who travelled round the south of England in 1661-3; he wrote an account of his travels which has been translated and published, indicating that some places like Norwich were standard tourist destinations after Charles II's restoration. Other travellers who supported the Protestant Prince of Orange later came to this country.

There were too few seventeenth century travel writings for Jeremy Black to include them in his book about the Grand Tour, while he found a large number of eighteenth century accounts, both published and unpublished. His comprehensive research emphasises the value of Walker's travels in the 1670s. John Walker travelled to parts of Britain not often the target of English travellers; his view of both Wales and Scotland contrasted their relative poverty with that of his home country, a view echoed in the following century by those English travellers who ventured to cross the English borders. His journeys to France preceded the hostilities which would follow from the Protestant William of Orange's successful replacement of James II on the English throne, which deterred though did not completely prevent some English men from travelling through the country. Walker's attitude to the French, however, was vividly uncomplimentary, although he admired the wealth of royal displays, and expressed no actual criticism of the French king's disregard for the citizens of Paris in demolishing 1000 houses to create the Louvre.[19] Walker possibly decided not to go to Italy because of his aversion to Roman Catholicism.[20] His travels in the later seventeenth century are therefore particularly valuable both for their descriptions and for their general comments.

His classical education gave him a strong interest in Latin inscriptions wherever her found them, and also in the Roman antiquities which he admired in Provence. He thought the natives of the cities like Nimes and Arles not very knowledgeable about their extraordinary monuments. In a number of places,

---

18   Esther Moir, *The Discovery of Britain. The English tourists. (1964). John Taylor, Travels and Travelling 1616-1653 ed J Chandler (enlarged edition, Hobnob Press 2020).*

19   See Walker's first journey, apropos Ghent.

20   Black, *the Grand Tour, 1-3.*

however, he found guide books describing churches and other sights of interest to travellers. A particular moment was his admiration for the Pont du Gard. Moreover he was sufficiently well-informed not only about the Roman past, but also on the fashions of art to reflect a surprising moment of admiration for the 'goodly landskips of hills and forrest worke' which he saw through the arches while sitting on horseback.

Why did John Walker decide to write accounts of his journeys? He seems to have written the accounts at a later date, referring occasionally to his memory or 'as neeere as I remember' to certain details. He had kept notes written at the time, mentioning when writing about Nimes in France that 'The cursoriness of my notes' nearly led him to omit the description of some 'rarities' he had seen. In the 1670s he was not yet married and did not have a son to whom he could pass the accounts; possibly he wrote them after 1692 when he was married and subsequently had two sons but if so he did not insert information current at that later date. He might have intended to pass his accounts to his relatives, or to his colleagues in London.

Did he have any idea of publishing the material? He sometimes wrote as though he were preparing a guide book and referred more than once to the 'reader'. The political observations Walker made both in this country and abroad show a sharp appreciation of the constitution of his home country and one of his most interesting observations was his analysis of the poor state of the French peasantry, identifying some hundred years before the French Revolution what would eventually lead to the dramatic events of 1789.[21]

The accounts also show how interested he was in the economic possibilities of harbours and maybe he wrote up his journeys in order to have ready to hand his views of where merchants might find opportunites. His accounts of his travels reveal an interest in the economy of the various towns he visited, and possibly he was a merchant as well as Chief Usher of the Exchequer; his own son was certainly apprenticed as a merchant.[22] His comments show a caste of mind which was rather different from that of Thomas Baskerville, another traveller in later Stuart Engand whose writings have been published; Baskerville's interests were in working situations rather than the more theoretical trading opportunities he encountered.[23] But these suggestions about Walker's particular interests can only be speculative.

In this respect Walker's commercial interest was similar to that of

---

21 See journey 8, 'Rhone', where he addresses the 'Reader'.
22 SHC/DD/WHb/70.
23 *Thomas Baskerville: Travels in Industrious England, ed Anthea Jones (Hobnob Press, 2023).*

Celia Fiennes, who at the end of the century set out on her journeys through England, writing up her notes for the benefit of her family. Though Walker was unlikely to have known about her travel journals, he certainly had some knowledge of her family: her father, Colonel Nathaniel Fiennes, had been accused by Clement Walker of cowardice in failing to defend Bristol vigorously enough against Prince Rupert in July 1643. Briefly imprisoned by the House of Lords, Walker was released to pursue charges against Fiennes, who was courtmartialled and condemned to death; he was pardoned by his commander the Earl of Essex.[24] The divisions of the civil war would have been clearly known though distant from the personal experiences of both Celia Fiennes and John Walker. Celia Fiennes shared with Thomas Baskerville, another traveller in later Stuart Engand whose writings have been published, a marked interest also in how things were grown and made, a caste of mind which Walker did not generally display. Baskerville was interested in working situations rather than the more theoretical trading opportunities he might have encountered.[25]

Celia Fiennes' travels, she said, were to recover her health. Walker's travels were perhaps simply to occupy his time in an interesting way and avoid the country gentleman's tendency to slothfulness.

Twenty-one pages at the reverse end of the Commonplace book

WALKER COVERED 21 pages of writing at the reverse end of the Commonplace book, as has already been referred to above. There are copies of a number of legal documents concerning the office of Chief Usher, some documents relating to property rights, but most are concerned with political affairs especially in 1673 and the parliamentary concern with the Roman Catholicism of Charles II's brother, James. Walker also copied out the Humble Petition and Advice which had been presented to Oliver Cromwell in 1657. It is interesting that he examined this formal statement of the English constitution; it had led to Cromwell refusing the title of King while acepting the traditional duties and position of kingship, while in name simply 'Lord Protector'. The Petition contained clear statements of the traditional constitution of two houses of parliament, lords and commons, of the existence of a Privy Council, and of the duty of the Lord Protector 'to uphold, and maintain the true Reformed Protestant Christian Religion, in the purity thereof, as it is contained in the Holy Scriptures of the Old and New Testament'. It provided Walker with arguments to back up his position.

24 ODNB.
25 *Thomas Baskerville: Travels in Industrious England, ed Anthea Jones (Hobnob Press, 2023).*

Correspondence concerning publication of the Commonplace book

THE BLACK LEATHER box in which John Walker's commonplace book is safely stored contains a label 'From Mrs Walker Heneage, Coker Court, Yeovil, Somerset.' Stored in it also is a typed transcript of Walker's accounts of his travels, which did not pay heed to Vita Sackville West's very appropriate comment on Walker's use of abbreviations. It also contains correspondence, including a letter from Virginia Woolf headed Hogarth Press, three letters from Vita Sackville West, regarding attempts to have the travel accounts published in 1931, and the receipt for typing the transcript, which was done in 1938 and showed an intention to secure publication.[26]

Dorothy Heneage, wife of Godfrey Heneage of Coker Court, was the proponent of the scheme to publish the travel accounts, which she described as a diary. She was a friend of Vita Sackville West, who addressed her with characteristic enthusiastic affection. The diary was lent to Vita, who then intended to show it to the Woolfs. She wrote to 'Dearest Dorothy' from Sissinghurst Castle and from Long Barn in the Weald, Sevenoaks in 1931. She was astute in her appraisal of Walker's writing, suggesting to Dorothy that it would be a good idea to modernise the abbreviations used by Walker, as 'they make it slightly irritating to read', a verdict with which this editor agrees.

The Woolfs took some time to consider whether the Hogarth Press might publish it. Virginia's verdict in November 1931 was polite in her response, but she thought it 'of too little general interest to appeal to the ordinary public'. At the distance of three hundred and fifty years, the rarity of travel journals of the seventeenth century, and the wide range of his travels, make John Walker's accounts more valuable and interesting than they seemed in 1931.[27]

Editing John Walker's travel diaries

THESE TEN TRAVEL accounts were written by John Walker himself and the handwriting and orthography are very consistent. As indicated above, Walker made use of notes he kept while travelling. On a very few occasions he

---

26 There is a brief account of John Walker's life within this group of papers which erroniously identified him with his older sibling, also called John.

27 John Walker's description of the way in which the grass on the site of Sir Charles Lucas' execution in Colchester was carefully prevented from regrowing in order to encourage royalist tourists then going to the town was contributed by Somerset Heritage Centre to the volume of then unpublished travel writings for *The Observant Traveller,* ed Robin Gard (HMSO 1989) and led to exploration of the rest of the John Walker material.

copied a few words twice from his notes, or left out some wording which he had to squeeze in.

Walker had a formal and slightly mannered style of handwriting seen for example in the letter 'W' written with quite elaborate curlicues. The initial letter of a great many words could be interpreted as a capital letter, as it was larger than the rest of the word, and this applied to all parts of speech; it was not possible to see any clear principle in his usage but rather his style was to start writing a word with a minor flourish. On the other hand, proper names often did not start with a larger letter, and this applies to places as well as persons, which suggests that the larger letters were not an important distinction. 'Paris', for example, is always clearly written as 'paris'. Nor did Walker usually start a sentence with a noticeably larger or capital letter as is the modern practice. As many sentences started 'ye' for 'the', as with 'p' it seems there was no capital letter available. The editor has therefore adopted modern practice as far as possible on capitalisation.

The punctuation has rarely needed alteration. Walker used the modern range: colon, semi-colon, comma and full stop. With a text written with a quill pen 350 years ago, the interpretation of a full-stop can be problemmatic, and Walker sometimes used a semi-colon where now a full stop would be used, so that in a few instances the punctuation has been modernised. In other cases, a word at the beginning of a line, although without a preceding full stop and without a capital letter, did sometimes clearly indicate the start of a new sentence. Walker did not usually employ a possessive apostrophe and one has not been inserted by the editor. He divided the text into paragraphs and mainly inserted headings above each main tourist experience, although in the interests of clarity a new paragraph has occasionally been inserted by the editor.

There has been no editing of Walker's spelling. Where his orthography varies from modern practice it is clear what the word is. Spelling is not quite consistent throughout, so that a frequently used word like 'verry' is usually written with two 'r's' but now and again is written as today with one. There was a practice of doubling 'l' at the end of words, and very often adding an 'e' to the end of a word where one would no longer be added.

Although the spelling of many place-names is not as used today, names are generally clear and a footnote has not been added to give the modern version of the name. Only in those cases where the name may not be readily recognised has a modern version been indicated. Walker himself recognised in his first account of a journey that '(for wanting the language we did often mistake)' the names of places.

Many abbreviations were used in the text, and these have been expanded by the editor. Thorn, 'y', was used almost always: ye (the), ym (them), yn (then), ys (this), yt (that); he sometimes wrote 'yu' with the 'u' raised above the line, which might be interpreted as 'thou' but has been taken here to be 'you'. Walker almost invariably abbreviated 'which' to 'wch'. Other words might be abbreviated, like 'agt' for 'against'. He indicated a double 'm' with a line on top of the m, but spelled 'midle' with one 'm' and no line on top. Instead of an ending in 'ed' for a past tense, Walker nearly always omitted the 'e' and put instead an apostrophe before the 'd'. He liked to quote Latin inscriptions, and these and other foreign words are italicised. He used what appears to have been a standard abbreviation for the ending of many of the Latin words in the inscriptions which he copied down: it appears as 'bg' and was apparently a shortened version of *'bus'*.

Travelling in France, Walker often mentioned the name of the administrative area he had reached, mainly an historic province, commenting also if a town were the capital, and this is helpful in mapping the course of his journeys. France was divided into many and varied administrative areas, all swept away in 1789 and new tidy divisions into departments and districts introduced; the old provinces disappeared in 1791. There has since been some further reorganisation. Thirty-six historic divisions into government areas were not necessarily coterminus with the provinces but shared their names and are accepted as reflecting the historic provinces.

Walker's spelling of the more important towns' names is generally close to the modern spelling, and he may well have had a map to guide him. The modern form of many of the French place-names he mentioned is footnoted and also indexed, his spelling where different indicated in brackets. Palaces and chateaux named by Walker are indexed, but not personal names, with some exceptions like relations of the king of France.

In Great Britain, Walker often identified the county he was visiting, in Wales using county names as headings, but here, too, boundaries have since been reorganised. The modern form of place-names, where not easily identified, has been given in footnotes and all places mentioned are indexed, although Walker's comment on some was extremely brief, with Walker's spellings also given in brackets. Houses which he named have been indexed but not personal names.

I

A VOYAGE TO THE NETHERLANDS

A Voyage begunn in August Anno 1671

ON THE 5TH of this Instant we took boat for Gravesend and on the same day about 4 of the clock in the afternoone we imbarq't in a Dutch vessel (cal'd the Golden Fortune) and anchor'd that night in Leigh Road. Next morning early we sett saile with a strong westerly wind. The sea being somwhat tempestuous we were (all the morning) delighted with the playing of porposes. It continued a stiff gale till 12 of the clock the 7th of this Instant, about which time we came into the Maze[1] a delightfull, commodious river. We left the Brill (a Cautionary towne[2] formerly in the hands of the English) on the right hand, and about 5 of the clock in the afternoone arriv'd at Rotterdam.

Rotterdam

IT WAS OUR fortune to come here in the Kermass (or faire time) where we beheld the splendor, and opulency of the place their Train-Bands (as we may call them) were then exercising, or skirmishing from streete, they all fire with a Rest, according to the old way. Most of their musqueteers were verry stately in their coslets, and headpieces of silver. The towne is large, and of great trade; the Grafts[3] verry commodious for receiving of small vessells. Here allwayes harbour some of the greatest Men of Warr belonging to the States. Erasmus is saide to have receiv'd his birth here, in whose memory they have erected a statue of brass on their chief-bridge, and his encomium in two latine distichs on the house where he was born. In this towne is likewise the residence of a Dike-Grave, or Conservator of the Banks, who sits every Tuesday in a stately structure cal'd the Cammene-Lond House, somthing like our Assizes,

---

1 River Meuse.
2 Brill (Brielle) by the 1585 <u>Treaty of Nonsuch</u> was one of three Dutch towns occupied by the English while intervening in the war against Spain. The towns were returned to the Dutch Republic in 1616.
3 *Graft* is a canal.

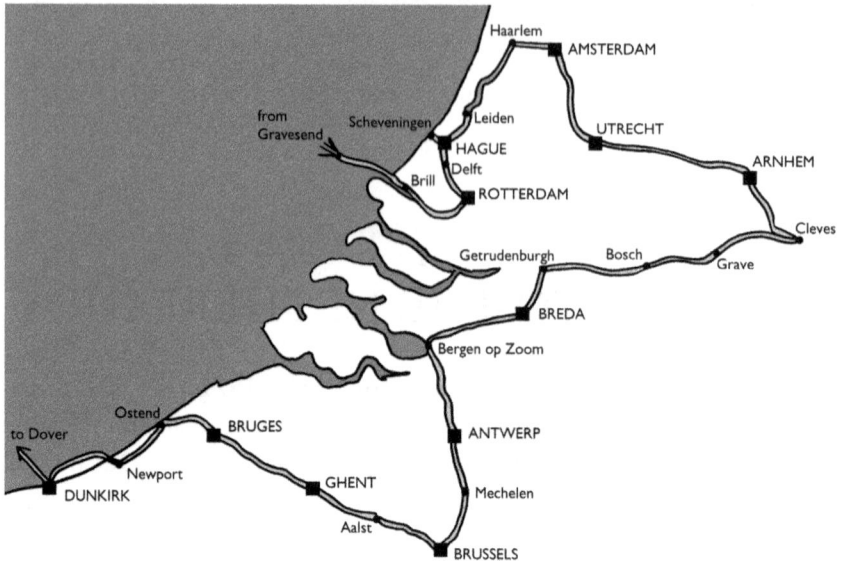

and gives judgment in all causes of meum, and tuum, within the extent of his Jurisdiction.

> *Ædibus his ortus Mundum decoravit Erasmus*
> *Antibus Ingenio, Religione Fide*
> *Fatalis Series nobis invidit Erasmum*
> *Sed Desiderium tollere non potuit.*

August 8th. We took boate for Delf, and passt through a litle dorp cal'd Overschee.[4] This citty is neatly built and extreamly delightfull, lying upon rising ground; the Grafts are cleere, and free from all noy-somness, a place of pleasure, wrather than trade, full of rich inhabitants. In the chief church we saw the tombs of William of Nassaue prince of Orange who was assassinated in this towne, and of Vantrump who was slain in an ingagement at sea against the English.[5] The Stat-House is an elegant structure. In the open space betweene this, and the Great-Church, is kept a tame eagle; which (according to report) they are oblig'd to by their Charter. Our passage from Rotterdam hither stood us in four stivers[6] apiece.

4   Delft; Overschie.
5   William of Nassau or William the Silent of Orange was assassinated in 1584. Maarten van Tromp died in 1653.
6   The stuiver was the smallest Dutch coin, worth 5 cents.

Hague

AUGUST 9TH. FROM hence we went by water to the Hague, the largest dorp, or village in all Holland. This place is famous for the Assembly of the States Generall, as also for the States of Holland; the place of their meeting in consultations is the Hoff, or Court. The roome of the States of Holland is verry rich, and stately I think litle inferior to some of the most exquisite roomes in Europe.

Here are severall remarkable buildings, amongst which is the house of prince Morrice, and that of the princess dowager in the Bosch, or wood: nor is the New-Church here less observable, being of a verry exact, and commodious model, capacious enough for 4, or 5 thousand persons in a small space. Opdams tomb[7] with his glosing epitaph in the Great-Church may afford good diversion to most Englishmen. Our curiosity drew us likewise to see the Long Walk cutt through the Sandy-Hills to Schevling[8] lying upon the open sea.

Leyden

AUGUST 10TH. In the afternoone we left the Hague, and passt along a delightfull channel to Leyden the most famous university in all the States Dominions, the approach to this citty is besett with banquetting-houses, and a grove on the right hand which affords great variety to travellers. It is large, and well fortified. About the midle of the towne stands a Burgh, or round Mount which (they say) was first raiss'd by the Saxon Hengist. This by means of a well in it, when the Spaniard beleguer'd the towne held out incredibly, and was at last the occasion of raising the siege. Here is a fair-church dedicated to St Peter. The Anatomy Schoole is full of Egyptian, and Roman antiquities. The Physic Garden is but small but affording sufficient variety for the best herbarist. The students are not here confin'd to formalities as they are in Oxford, but left to their liberty both for their habit, and recreations.

Harleim[9]

ON THE 11TH of this Instant we went by water to Harleim where we view'd the most beautifull, and largest church in all Holland. They report that the Harlemites formerly gave assistance to Barbarossa the Africk king in the taking of Damietta in Egypt from the Saracens, and that they brought away two bells of Corinthian-brass as a trophy of their honour; these they refus'd

7   Jacob van Wassenaer Obdam, a Dutch Admiral killed in action.
8   Scheveningen.
9   Haarlem.

to show us because some pilfering French-man going up to see them hade conveyed away the clapper. Here we observ'd the custome of their buriall, the women never follow the corps to the grave. This towne has been once, or twise fir'd, carelessly leaving boules of tobacco about in places, insomuch that the taking of it in publick is prohibited under great penalty. They boast that the invention of printing was first discovered amongst them.

Amstelodam[10]

AMSTELODAM THE METROPOLIS of all Holland was the next place we came to. A citty of a boggy, and unwholsome scituation: but extreme populous, and large; so that I conceive it litle inferior to London; and in the Heere-Graft[11] and some other parts thereof farr exceeding in building. Many of the merchants houses are of the Corinthian order (in imitation of the Italians) the lower roomes generally pav'd with marble, and on the top batlements sett with figures; insomuch that is usuall to lay out tenn, or twelve thousand pound sterling upon a single house. On the 12th our curiosity was diverted with a sight of the Stat House a verry costly work, the inside is illustrated with variety of painting, and carv'd marble; but the frontispiece comes farr short of the rest of the work. Yet the Duch have this salvo for it, that it was contriv'd for strength as well as beauty, there chief bank being lodg'd within it. If any be so curious to inquire farther into this structure, he may procure the Book of Cutts of the severall places, and roomes belonging to it.

Their Burse is but meane, and no way to be reckon'd with the worst of our Exchanges; but the trade of the towne is so great, one would think the wealth of the world were brought hither. Here are Hospitalls for all sorts, and sexes; for they think nothing more pernicious to the Goverment than to suffer the meaner sort of people to live in idleness. The chimes goe verry delightfully most part of the day: and about 7 of the clock in the evening the organists repaire to their respective churches, and play all variety of tunes to divert, and recreate the people: it is usuall to have two, or three of this sort of instruments in every church. In the New-Church we beheld a most glorious skreene of burnisht brass, and a pulpit (which they say) stood them in 1500£ the carving. Brass lavers or fonts are frequent with them running up into a pyramid of great height; this towne affords you a rellish of all religions, amongst which is a famous Jewish Synagogue. The natives throughout Holland are for the most part <are> Calvenists, their ministers are allow'd of, and paid their salary by the States Generall, and in case they are dislik't they

10 Amsterdam.
11 Herengracht

send 'um their wayes, with a new-pare of shooes; which is a certain signe they are discharg'd from their cure.

The inconveniencies of this place are many; but one of the chiefest is that they have no fresh water but what descends from heaven, which they are forc't to preserve under ground in litle brick-houses plaister'd with paris: they admitt of few coaches upon wheeles for feare of shaking, and loosning the foundations but sliding in the manner of our sledges at Bristoll, no building any where without piles. The grafts for the most part smell noysome in a morning, but custome makes in [it?] naturall to the inhabitants. They are verry strict in their laws, yet have they severall licentious houses, as the Longen Celdur, or long cellar, which is the Terpaulins Whetstones park, where they meet every night betweene 7 and 9 and truck for love, or money. 3 or 4 stivers is a common price for a doxy. We lodg'd at an Englishmans (one Browne, who liv'd over against the Ode Kirk[12]) and made the observation that we were more impos'd upon by our owne cuntrymen than any other persons.

On the 16th we left this place and went by boate to Utricht[13] being 8 hours passage from Amstelodam. Hitherto we found a verry flat cuntry the product whereof was litle else but light oats, and sedgie-grass, but here we found a great alteration. The towne lies upon rising ground vested with a wholesome serene aire; great store of orchards gardens, and corn-fields lying about it. Here was formerly a fine Mal[14], but now fallen to decay. The grafts lie verry deepe, and low so that their kitchins, washouses, and out-offices in most places lie under the streets, and cloose to the water. They show'd us an old-church on one of the columns whereof was the picture of a black bull, with this distich by him.

Accipe posteritas tua qd pr sæcula narres
Tourinis Cutibus fundo solidata Columna est

It seems in digging the foundation some springs burst forth, which hindered the artificers, but an old man was admonisht in a dreame to advise 'um to lay beasts hides under it, which they did and proceeded in the work. This is a university of note, and many resort hither for the conveniency of the aire, but it does not come neere Leyden for number of students.

The next morning early we hir'd a waggon (with three horses a brest) for Arnham[15] which was a long dayes journey, being in all twelve houres

12 Oude Kirk.
13 Utrecht.
14 An avenue. The word is used quite often in the text.
15 Arnhem.

passage, for the most part of the morning we travel'd through a fruitfull cuntry, orchards lying thick on both hands of us for severall miles together; planted with abundance of Burgamy-pares, aples, plums and such like. Towards the midle of the day we came to the towne of Rhene[16] denominated (as I suppose) from the river, being upon the utmost borders of the province of Utricht, whither the King of Bohemia (who married the daughter of King James of England) fled after he was deposed by the Emperor, and so enter'd the Dutchy of Gelderland, the States whereof hold the first place in the Assembly of the States Generall. The cuntry is greatly barren, and hilly (like Windezore Forrest[17]) and so continu'd till we came to Arnham a verry antient towne, the metropolis of the Dutchy, and lying upon the River Rhine, it is inviron'd with an old fortification. Here we beheld a faire church with a tomb of the former Dukes of Geldenland.

On the 18th we sett forward on our journey, and pass't through a small towne cal'd Huesden,[18] and so entred the Duke of Brannenburghs territories:[19] here we found the people verry poore most of them waring seboes on their feet like the French peasants, and the children standing upon their heads, and begging in the high-wayes. We ferried over the Rhine where we saw a litle Man of Warr crusing about to demand tribute (for the States) of the boates that passt too, and froe in the river; for the streame is not so rapid here (as some conceive) but that they saile up in a dry season with an indifferent gale of wind. Being come opposite, our phansie led us to take a view of Kinkensconce (an island under the dominion of the States) which divides the Rhene into two branches, one whereof is cal'd the Vaal; after some small stay here we obtain'd leave (by an English souldier] to take a view of the Works, which were so exactly made that we conceiv'd the place allmost impregnable.

By the evening we reacht Cleve in Germany, an old towne scituate upon a hill, with a verry delighfull cuntry round it, on one of the gates whereof was the picture of Eumeus the famous rhetorician.[20] Here is a large antient castle, which is somtimes made the residence of the Dukes of Brannenburgh the principall roomes whereof (were at this time) furnished with guilded leather; but the glory of all was that there belonged to it the most pleasant park that ever we beheld. Here prince Morrice of Nassau kept a verry delicate stable of

16 Rhenen; the Rhine river.
17 Windsor Forest?
18 Heusden.
19 Brandenburg.
20 Is this a reference to Eumaeus the swineherd in the Odyssey?

horses. In the towne by permission was a poore clyster of Franciscans, and another of Capuchines, as likewise a small nunnery of lay-sisters that gott a lively-hood by weaving.

This being the 19th we took waggon for the Grave, being about 6 houres travel distant from Cleve.[21] This is a frontiere towne in Brabant under the command of the States Generall; but the prince of Orange is the proprietor. It lies upon the Moze, a low cuntry about it; but exceedingly fortified and all with turf. Here likewise a house of Bagans, or poore lay-nuns.

Hence on the 20th we proceeded by waggon to the Bosch another frontiere towne in Brabant, spatious, and well garrison'd; once a Cautionary to the English. We were conducted about the walls by a Scotch souldier in the States service; as we were walking about here, we observ'd severall riding the ring, and other postures; for though the troopers are but indifferently horst, yet they are all brought to the Mannage.[22] Upon our entring into this towne, as at the Grave we gave in our names to the Governor. We dieted, and lodg'd here well, and reasonably, and went off early the next morning.

This being the one and twentieth, (finding we were like to be impos'd upon by the waggoners) we diverted our course, and took places in a Greate Scute (or boate)[23] with many other passengers bound for Dort in Holland. We went through a litle dorp cal'd Guercombe, and so into the river Moze[24], and arrived time enough to take an indifferent prospect of the towne before night. Tis large, and for a long time continued the Staple of trade; but is now much drained by Rotterdam. All the lands lying about it are imployed by whitsters[25] of linning cloth. Here are two doulyes or taverns one whereof is the place in which the Synod of Dort sate which broacht the doctrine of Arminius. The other was built by the Earle of Leicester, and still retains the arms of England upon the gates. The Mint, or principle coining-house of the States is here: though for the most part they stamp as bad money as any in Europe. viz: doits. 8-1d stivers 1d double stivers 2d, and shillings which is nothing but copper slightly washt over. All the good coine that goes amongst 'um is either Spannish or German money.

21 Cleves.
22 Manège, the french word for a Riding Academy.
23 Escute, a Flemish boat like a wide rowing boat used in the marshes.
24 Gorinchem also spelled Gorkum. Moze i.e. the river Meuse.
25 Bleachers of linen cloth.

Bredah[26]

W E DEPARTED HENCE on the 22nd and sail'd on the Moze to
Getrudenburgh, so into Brabant to the pleasant towne of Bredah
noted for holding out a twelve months siege against the Spaniard under
Marquess Spinola though at last surrendred. It ha's labor'd under various
revolutions of fortune, having been often taken, and retaken; but 'tis now
wholy subjected to the Dutch. Most of the houses belong to the Prince
of Orange together with a verry vast castle wherein the King of Englands
commissioners concluded that dishonorable treaty with the States in the
yeare 1667. In the midle of the towne stands a goodly church with a well-
carv'd monument erected in honour of Grave Henry of Nassau: four antient
heroes supporting his warlick trophies. The tower belonging to this church
is of a prodigious height, and gives a large prospect into all the neighboring
townes and villages. We hir'd a waggon and wrode out some three miles
from the towne to take a view of a verry stately wood of pines belonging
to the prince being at least 6 miles in compass: here we were divertiz'd with
severall bickerings betweene the rookes, and herns.[27] All the land hereabout
is delicately planted, and sett with severall rows of trees.

From hence on the 23rd we went by waggon to Berghemop-Zome[28]
being 7 houres journey, wherein was litle remarkable but the invincible
Works of the towne. This is likewise a frontiere in Brabant belonging to the
States. We now quitted the States Dominions, and on the 24th (by waggon)
journeyed towards Antwerpe; seated in a wide plaine upon the banks of the
river Scaldis,[29] showing so many princely structures, and lofty towers, that
all passengers approach it with as much pleasure as if they were going to
contemplate the greatest beauty, or paramor in the world. Our hire hither
stood us in 10 guilders. Our horses tir'd within 2 hours after we sett out:
but the citty comming within our prospect it soone mitigated all other
inconveniencies. About the evening we entred and took up our lodging at the
Rose-Noble.

In the first place we went to look upon the walls, and fortifications of
the towne, than which nothing of so much strength bares a greater proportion
of neatness: on the top are verry delightfull walkes sett with severall rows of
trees. Beneath at the foot of these walkes (in the summer evenings) the ladies

26 Breda.
27 Heron?
28 Bergen op Zoom.
29 Scheldt river.

come out to aire themselves in their coaches; so that they that walke above (have) at the same time a double advantage of prospect; on the one hand the pleasure, and delight of the cuntry, on the other the gallantry, and bravery of the gentry. Eight, or nine greate gates of the Dorick order. A citadel compos'd of five bastions of wonderfull curiosity, and strength; as we passt over the bridge to it stood a shrine of the Virgin Mary in a Watch-House. Devotion raigns somuch in this towne that we found severall of the Spannish souldiers as they complemented show'd a litle crucifix pasted in the inside of their hatts. The citty is about 6 miles in compass, the streets ample and spatious, adorn'd with many figures sett up for piety and veneration. The trade of this place would be exceeding greate but that the Dutch obstruct it who have two forts lower upon the river, which take an accompt of all vessells that pass up to the citty. The houses belonging to the merchants, and gentry are most commonly large, and stone-built with faire gardens of greate curiosity belonging to 'um.

Tis a strange company of painters that are here resident, but most of their pieces are either pictures of saints, crucifixes, or shrines to the Virgin. In some of their chief churches we saw many paintings of Rubens, and Michael Angelo's. Some shrines of the Virgin all of massy silver with a circle of angels (of the same) adorning it. The Jesuites college here is a structure of the greatest admiration that ever I yet look't upon, the altars all of spotted marble wav'd about in lively vaines, the pavement of black, and white marble, the columes, and batlements of asiatick marble. The confession seats exquisitely carv'd with cherubims. The roof richly guilded, and painted by Ruben and Brugelius. In the church dedicated to the Virgin Mary is a tablet of greate rarity, drawne by a black-smith of this towne, expressing the fight of Michael and his angels with the bad spirits. Father Worsely the English Jesuite show'd us the library and the rest of the college. From hence we betook our selves to the house of the Friers Canius[30] a handsome building with fountains in the courts. Afterwards we went to the English nunnery; they are of the order of Tiresians, they live very strict, eate nothing but flesh, were no stockins, only sandalls upon their feete. At the Grate we convers'd with 2 Sisters (both profest nuns) of the family of the Wakemans in Glocestershire, they entertain'd us with a pretty kind of story how their patroness the Lady Tiresia had confer'd a peculiar gift upon their Order which was that none of them should ever harbour any vermin, which wee lookt upon as a verry heavenly favour. The citizens wives are usually of a good handsome straine & verry curteous; they ware a thing plaited like a vaile (which is cal'd a heuke) with a tassell bending out from their foreheads

30 Possibly a reference to a religious foundation by Peter Canisius (1521-1597), a Catholic reformer who was a Jesuit.

in manner of our hawks hoods. Here we remain'd to the 26th, and so took waggon for Mechlin.[31]

We din'd at Mechlin a neate, pleasant towne and an episcopall see, with a faire church dedicated to St Rumbald and on the 27th being Sunday arrived in a waggon at Bruxells[32], the usuall seate of the Governors of the Spannish Netherlands, which is thought most commodious being in Brabant and edging upon the borders of Flanders; it is of a great extent the streets ly steepe, and rising; yet spatious and well beautified with fountains, and aquæducts, the principall whereof is the Mannicke piss[33]: being the figure of a brass boy erected upon a pedestall; the water issuing from his privy member (at a good distance) into a stone cistern, or receiver. The pallace, or Residence of the Governors is an antient, sollid building, resembling this at White Hall, but with more curiosity, excepting the part of the Banqueting House. At the front of the pallace you come upon a broade space incircl'd with pillars, and rare carv'd stone work; on the top whereof (heretofore) stood many brass figures. But the avarice of some of their Governors ha's now reduc'd 'um only to 4: 2 whereof are those of Albertus and Isabella.

Entring the pallace on the left hand stood an Old Hall with shops, allmost like that at the Hage. Belonging to it is a verry sumptuous chappel, and a gallery full of images of severall of the Austrian, and Burgundian families. Hence we were ledd into the parke, which well wooded but not so large as St James's; here is a canal pav'd on each side and at the bottom with smooth broade stone, many artificiall rocks streaming with water, some of them composed of the roots, or stumps of trees. But that which most rare, and delightfull was a retiring place of the Archduchess Isabella, wherein was a rock sett with shells, and mother of pearle, a water organ affording great harmony, the tritons, or sea-gods sounding their hollow shells, all sorts of artificers at work. Swanns and other fowle swimming about in a circle, with a neate devise of 2 bells running upon a string from one dragons mouth to another, and last the water springing out of litle holes in the pavement, and so falling downe like a shower of raine all which was perform'd to the greate admiration of the spectators. After this we betook our selves to Count Marsins pallace (then Generall of the Horse) heretofore the Court of the Nassau's; part of it lies ruinous having been (a few years since) beate downe by a thunder stone which brought so much sulphur and combustible matter that it quickly consum'd the timber work, the stone hangs up at the gate in ribs of iron which I guesst to be about 150 pound.

31 Mechelen in Northern Belgium.

32 Brussels.

33 Manneken Pis.

In the open space before the Stat House they show'd us the place where Count Egmond, and Horn were beheaded upon which is erected a stately fountain. The Stat House is full of antient pictures, but that which is most priz'd is Solomons Judgment by Reuben valu'd at 4000 Florens.

After this we went to the Armory, where we beheld verry exquisite rarities, as bucklers, headpieces of carv'd and stain'd work, coats of male swords pistolls and gunns of admirable art. The skinn of the white horse which brought the Arch-duke Albert from the batle of Newport with a tablet of verses in his commendations. Another of a pie-bal'd colour which the Arch-duchess Isabella wrode on when she enter'd Bruxells in state both upon woodden frames. In all this variety we ought not to omitt a buckler of Charles the 5ths which he caus'd to be made for his night sports when he went in quest of his mistresses; in the inside was a dark lantern full of litle slouping holes, that if the adversary made any home pass upon the least turn of the arm he broke off his point, and at the same time might fall in and wound him with a short sword that stuck in the center of the buckler.

From these sæcular things we pass over to the religious. viz: to the English nunnery, at the Grate we discoursed with 2 nunns who bore the name of Russell; they were Augustines by Order, the Lady Wigmore was their Abbess. We went to heare their Vespers but found that they chanted so miserably we could hardly refraine laughing. In the chief church we saw an altar of the Carmelites, which show'd 'um to be amorous friers: the Virgin Mary was dress'd in the French mode, diverse finedress'd neate angells hanging in strings, and hovering over her: it put us in mind of Venus and her band of Cupids. After all we determin'd to goe without the towne, and take a view of the Works, we found it verry sandy in our walking as it is in all this part of Brabant: many of the bastions being growne defective, and mouldering away, were undertaken by the inhabitants whose diligence was verry observable here. At one bastion you might see the Jesuites at work, some digging, others wheeling, and filling the barrows. At another the Capuchins, and Franciscans imply'd after the same manner. At a third the Gentry and Marchants at worke in their holland wasecoats their ladyes sitting by in their coaches spectators of their lovers labours. All indeavoring to prevent the attacks of the French. To give further incouragement to this great proceeding the Governor of the Netherlands Count Mounterey a person of great conduct and management came attended with 4 trumpets and 40 horse nobly equip'd about 6 of the clock in the evening (according to his usuall custome) verry obligingly saluted the Religious, and the Gentry laboring at the severall bastions. This man by his singular diligence, ha's so secur'd all rodes, and passages, that Flanders which for a long time was reputed a denn of thieves; is now become as safe as any part of Europe and all in less than twelvemonths.

(Ghent)

O N THE 29TH we took waggon and came by dinner time to a neate litle towne cal'd Alhost[34] where we baited. We arrived here upon a Holy-day, the people in their best apparrel, their shops all shutt; that litle time we staide here we resolv'd to make use of in seeing the principall church, and observe the ceremonies of the festivall; knowing the priests and friers to have variety of tricks in all places. We no sooner entred this church and came up to the quire but we were presented with a rare show, the effigies of our Saviour in his purple robe sitting a stride upon a greate wooden ass, on the outside of the church He was standing under a small pent house with a taper burning by Him in the manner he was crucified, in his purple robe, and crowne of thorns upon his head. Having din'd we went our way for Ghent the largest citty in all the Spannish Netherlands; it is scituated in Flanders. The latines call it Gandavum, or Ganda. Here we found 'um as industriously repairing their fortifications as at Bruxels to keepe out those Locusts the French. Considering the magnitude of the place 'tis but thinly inhabited; the young women of the towne appear'd in a pretty antick dress in steeple-crown'd hats and long feathers hanging downe their wasts. Their State Huys is verry magnificent, in which were severall pourtraitures of Charles the 5th verry lively drawne one whereof was his rescuing a lady from the savage rage of a lyon. In the midle of the prime market place his statue is erected, and likewise that of Albertus and Isabella. This is noted for an English nunnery. We view'd the prime church which contain'd a multitude of stately chappels. In the tower is vast bell cal'd Rowland weighing above eleven thousand weight. The next day we departed from hence and proceeded on our journey to Bruges.

On the 30th Instant in the evening we reacht the delightfull towne of Bruges scituate in a flat plentifull part of Flanders: watered by the River Reya[35], a dark, and slow-running streame. Here (as at Ghent) we were not permitted to enter till we had given in our names. This towne represented to us greate variety of objects; many religious houses and churches. In that of the Virgin Mary we beheld an incomparable draught of Michael Angelo's showing Christ when he was taken downe from the Cross; a verry costly tombe in great brass-figures of the Duke, and Dutchess of Burgoine. A paire of exceeding large brass

34 Aalst, East Flanders, Belgium.
35 Reie river.

candlesticks standing before the altar in the quire above 12 foot in heighth. In this church is the effigies of St Christopher cutt out in stone of a wonderfull magnitude. After this we went to the Jesuites College who civilly show'd us the Library Schoole, and Theater and invited us to see the Tragedy of Martin Spira (acted by their young schollars the next day] but our occasions would not suffer us to tarry so long.

From hence we repair'd to the Abby of St Bartholomew or Bernard (for wanting the language we did often mistake) this we found to be a handsome regular building and a stately cloyster, here the [they?] show'd us the heads of 2 antient abbots Oswold, and Grimbold cast in silver, and of great proportion. The prior was verry respectfull to us, walkt about the garden, and presented us with grapes, and of her frutes sprigs of mertall [myrtle] and such like favours. But the obligations of the Lady Abbess of the English nunnery were above all things else. Her name was Brighurst, a comly well spoken woman. The house of the nunnery had been a pallace belonging to the Governours of the Netherlands a good old building. The Abbess favor'd us with a sight of some of her nunns amongst which was a sister of Sir Francis Englefields in Wiltshire. In the Chappel was buried the hart of the Lady Tenham of that family with an inscription over it. The Abbess being willing more and more to oblige us was pleased to grant us the favour to heare her quire of nunns; whilst we were discoursing a nunne came and tender'd her a key upon the knee, and after that wrose up and tould a bell, which was no sooner doune but we heard the nunns begann to convene in a gallery over head. After this we heard a most harmonious consort of viols, and violins, with the organ. Then the ravishing voice of a nunne singing in Italian a treble part alone; the rest now and then keeping the chorus. Next one of them plaide singly upon the lyre viol, and runne verry delighfull division. And last of all one of them plaide upon the trumpet marine to admiration. This favor was the greater because it was perform'd before the time of Vespers.

Having hitherto pleas'd our phansy with divine objects; we deem'd it not amiss to take a rellish of sæculars things in the Close. We walk't about the walls of the towne till we came to a place cal'd the Garden of the Archers viz: Hortus Sagittariorum. Twas indeede a verry curious waterwork, where all sort of artificers were at work as in that at Bruxels; on the outside of the railes are severall horsemen, their horses disgorging water, Neptune riding upon a dolphin. Fortune standing with one foot upon a globe, turn'd round all the time by the force of the waters; opposite to this is an archer standing with a drawne boe in his hand, the water ascending into his body and streaming out at the end of his arrow. In the midst of these knacks stood a bason with a golden ball in the midle which was forc't out of its center by a streame of water 10 or 12 foot high and so kept up for a long while; with diverse other pretty remarkable diversions. From hence we went off about 3 of the clock in the afternoone and took boate for Ostend.

Ostend

AFTER SOME DIFFICULTY in changing our boate two or three times we were at last brought safe to the litle towne of Ostend being about 5 houres from Bruges we lodg'd that night at one of our cuntrymens houses Tom Bales by name a drunken harmless fellow; we had not been long here when the souldiers came in to have us before the Governor, to whome we gave an accompt of ourselves and so were remitted to our lodging. Our entertainment here was homely, and indifferent, but to quallify it our charges were not unreasonable. The towne is for the most part the habitation of fishers salting, and drying of herrings and such like; but the strongest Hold throughout Europe having held out a siege against the Spaniards 3 years 3 months and 13 dayes till it was become a heape of rubbishe. From the tower of the Towne-House we view'd it you may see from walls to walls in every streete. We saw the House of the Capuchines and Sept 2nd took waggon for Newport. [The bottome 2 lines are squeezed onto the page]

Our passage betweene Ostend and Newport was in a verry whomely waggon, but delightfull being upon a plaine sand on the shore where we pickt up variety of color'd shells; the towne is but ordinary most of all depending upon the same trade as Ostend, here we baited and after dinner prepar'd to take boate; two of the souldiers undertook to carrie our portmantu's to the water side, but finding us strangers and wanting the Lingua they begann to exact; but one of the Spannish officers standing by and observing it took them as soone as ever they came out of the boate and can'd them severely. We rais'd our hatts to him for his greate civility and so went off from the towne.

In the boate we had the company of Father Patrick. After two houres we sail'd under a litle towne lying upon a knowle intrench'd and fortified (cal'd Fern) now in the possession of the French. We landed a mile before we came to Dunkirk the cutt reaching no nearer; being late we were constrain'd to be our owne porters, and carry our luggage through the sands up to the verry gates of the towne where we found all lock't fas't; and had we not had the Abbess of Ipres in our company (an English lady of the family of the Beaumonts in Leicestershire] we must of necessity have laide under the Sand-Works; but upon her prevalency we were had in a by way: 'twas my fortune by falling off from the Works to gett first into towne. We took up our Lodging that night at the Consenges the chief house of entertainment in the towne and in the roome where the king of France lodg'd his madamasels.

Our entertainments here was not to be dislik'd withall. In the roome where we sup'd the Magistrates (that day) had sate in judgment upon two malefactors that had stollen catle about Graveling[36], the custome is the extorct confession of the fact by straining of them hard upon a woodden sadle with cords fastned to their leggs. On the morrow we saw 'um severely scourg'd in the market-place the Magistrates sitting in a Bel-Cony [balcony] in the Stat-Huys and seeing execution fully perform'd: after they were whipt, they burn't them in the shoulders with a redd-hot iron, made 'um downe upon their knees to the Burgers and then rung the bell, and turn'd 'um out of the gates of the towne. Here is a faire church with a sumptuous altar, a neate chappel of the Jesuites, a House of Capuchins two small English nunneries, one of the Poore-Clares another of the Dames. In this of the Dames we saw two beautifull Irish ladies nuns, one was named Legg, the Abbess was of the family of the Carolls in Sussex.

The designe of a fortification here is greate but it was not neere finisht; severall large pieces of ordinance upon the Works, four hundred whereof were shamefully sold with the towne by the king of England to the French king. Here was one gunn of the king of France tooke from the Duke of Lorrain that was 28 foot in length. They were building here two frigats of 100 tunn apiece. The Cyclops were making of anchors, others twisting of ropes and cables: some working the engines to cleanse the harbor from sand. They refus'd to let us see the Cittadel. The night before we left the towne the Marquess D'Aumont Governor of Boloigne made his entry, and was saluted by the gunns round the towne, and took up his lodging at the Governors. Upon the 5th of 7br [September] we hir'd a waggon and took our journey for Graveling with Father Patrick.

We came to Graveling about 3 of the clock in the afternoone, having pass't by Mardike a demolisht fort; this is but a small place, but mightily fortified, the souldiers generally look't as if they were starv'd, death in their faces. Here is a large nunnery of Poore-Clares consisting of about four-score in number, the Abbess did us the favour to grant us a view of about 50 of them at their devotion at once; from hence we went directly to Calais that night, we left our valeses at the Custom House to be search't where the shirking French men made me pay for foule linning. Here we found verry badd accommodation and nothing but thieving, and exacting from a man in every corner. Here we saw the ceremony of a wedding, the priest dashing the bride with Holy-Water as if

36 Gravelines.

he would have put out her eyes; this occasion'd serenading for those 2 nights we were forc't to lodge in the towne. The towne ha's a double fortification that which the English built, and one made later by Cardinal Richleu. They refus'd here likewise to let us see the Cittadel, or the old Kisban [Kasbah] or castel built by the English, and lying upon the sands, or flats as you come into the towne. Having staide here 2 dayes the wind at last serv'd and we went off in the packet-boate and arrived safely at Dover (God be thanked) upon English ground again and so in two dayes came safe to London.

The motto under the Belgian lyon

Hac Libertatis Ergo.

Over the Physic Garden at Leyden

Presentam monstrat quolibet Herba Deum

2
A TRIP TO HOLMESDALE (REIGATE)

August 2nd 1672

I WENT TO see the castle of Holms-dale in Surrey by Rigate[37], whereof there is litle remaining but the ruines of a whimsicall building erected by the Lord Munson, the prospect from it is verry delightfull into a valley of the same name. Frome the brow of the hill where the castell stood we descended with lights in our hands into cave arch'd to a good height, and capacious, continuing thus quite through the sandy hills (above a furlong) which made it appeare like a rock on each side. By the whole frame of the thing I did conceive it had been made use off by the Saxons in nature of a sally port, which made 'um conceive it impregnable, as I guess by that old rhythme mention'd by Mr Cambden[38]

The Castle of Wholms-Dale
never wonne, nor never shall

---

37 Holmesday castle also called Reigate Castle. It was probably built about 1100, was in ruins by 1642 and totally demolished in 1648. Extensive earthworks remain, and the cave once below the castle, known as the 'Baron's cave'.

38 William Camden's *Britannia, a topographical and historical survey of England county by county,* was published in Latin in 1586, republished many times and first translated into English in 1610.

3

A JOURNEY TO NORWICH AND CAMBRIDGE

The headings have been added to the text at a later date; they are in a diffferent ink and hand and sometimes had to be squeezed in between the lines of the text.

August 20th 1672 Malden

WE TOOK OUR journey along the county of Essex to Rumford,[39] a litle before we came into the towne we saw a huge whale rib hung up in a frame of wood upon the highway from hence to Burnt-wood[40] and so to Malden that night. By the Romans stiled Camolodunum,[41] now a raggid old towne, with three parish churches; a litle Key to which small vessels of about threescore tunn come up; hard by it are some saltworks which is the principall trade of the towne. This place was raz'd by Queene Bodcea while in the hands of the Romans. There are yet greate remnants of their fortifications, the vallum and the agger being plainly to be perceiv'd all about it. About a mile from the towne stands Beale Abbey[42] which shows the ruines of a large cloyster but demollish'd with the rest upon the greate Reformation by Henry 8.

Colchester

THE NEXT DAY being the 21, we wrodd for Colchester, a greate towne but much ruin'd in the late Civil Warrs, the walls, and severall churches beaten downe by greate shott. The way for four, or five miles continu'd staitly

39 Romford.

40 Brentwood.

41 Walker was repeating the idea of Camden that Maldon was *Camolodunum*, though Leland thought that name related to Colchester. There are three churches in Maldon and salt is made there. Archaeologists have found evidence of a large ditched enclosure containing the burh. Maldon District Historical Environment Characterisation Project (Essex County Council, 2008), 107-8.

42 Beeleigh.

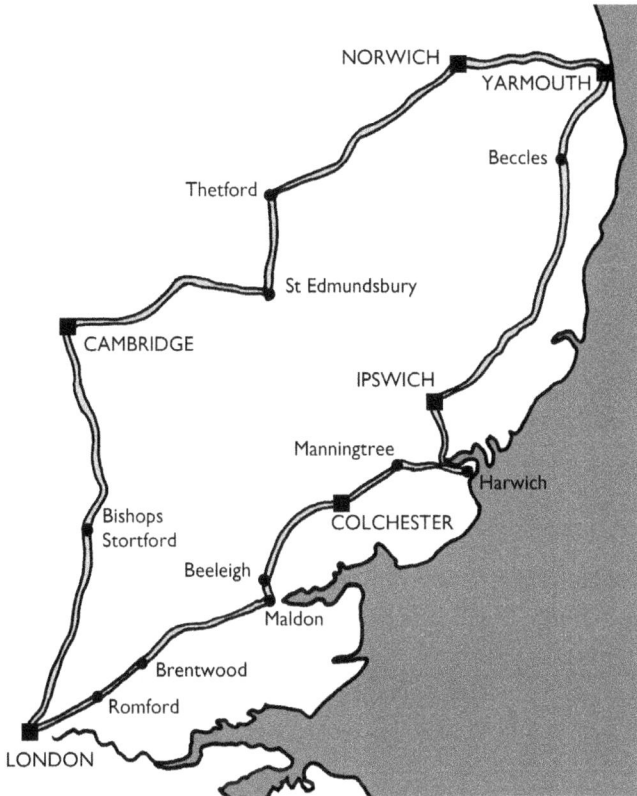

and open, but afterwards wooddy againe. We saw the remnant of the castle a square building with towers at each corner. This they say was rais'd by King Coel, or Coilus the founder of the tower; 'tis now in the possession of that wretched fellow Sir John Norfolk Serjeant to the House of Commons. The river which flows by it is cal'd Coln. We viewed the ruines of the Abby which was blowne up by the kings party (upon their surrender of the towne to the parlament) belonging then to the family of the Lucas's.

Neare to the Abby stands a small church wherein is inter'd Sir Charles Lucas who was shott to death upon the surrender of the towne in the late siege; there is put over him (by order of his brother the Lord Lucas) a stone with this inscription written in deepe ingrav'd characters that he was barbarously murder'd in cold blood by command of Sir Thomas Fairfax the Generall of the Parlament army. He was shott under the walls of the castle, and the Royallists carry on a cheate (as the papists did formerly) that the body works miracles, and has left a remarke of divine vengeance on the ground where it was shott, noe grass ever growing since, and remaining thus in the figure of a cross. But a litle boy told us that he had seene 'um poure scalding water upon it, therefore no wonder that it continu'd bare. Yet I cannot but think it strange that they should jugle at this rate to make saints of those that endeavour'd to overthrow the antient liberties of the people of England. The chiefe trade of this place is the manufacture of bayes, extreamly decayed since the happy Restauration (as they call it) here we din'd and so went to Mannitree[43], a litle towne belonging to fishers upon a small creeke where we took up our lodging that night.

Harwich

O N THE 22D in the morning we proceeded to Harwich being an ill rode, the place has some slight remmnants of a turf fortification, cast up about the time of the Dutch fight. A litle towne, and generally a raggid irregular building, the harbour verry commodious being for the most part tenn fathom in water. We ferried over on Suffolk side to view Landguard Fort lying upon a wide beech consisting of four bastions of earth made so ill that they annoy one another the trench allmost dry, the platforms ruinous. Here they show'd a litle Armory of musquets and bray'd mightily of it. All the ordenances were iron and some of them so decayed not likely to hold thrice firing, about 50 in number and ill mounted. This fort was first erected by the Earle of Warwick the parlament Admirall. Sir Charles Litleton was Commander at this time. We pickt up severall shells upon the beech and so retourn'd for Harwich. About 3 of the clock in the afternoone we had news brought us that our Admirall was discover'd sailing by to the boy of the Nore. We descri'd 'um afterward from the banks of the towne. The place affords but meane accommodation both for horse and man. Colonel Butler commanded a Foot Company here. We left it about five in the afternoon and with our horses (at a deare rate) ferried over to the Suffolk Coast and went that night for Ipswich.

Ipswich

T HIS TOWNE HA'S a faire scituation in a plaine cuntry upon a branch of the sea; so that formerly it had greate traffick; but now partaking of the misfortune of the negligence of the Goverment 'tis fallen to decay as most of the townes of England. 'Tis nigh two miles in building every way, faire streets, and severall gracefull buildings, the Goverment is by Bayliffs, Portmen and a Councel; 12 parish churches. Here is yet us'd some litle manufacture of broad cloth. At our being here the people labor'd under a greate oppression, eight Companies of Scotch were quarter'd upon 'um, and had not paid a penny in above two months, yet the people gave this character of them that they were indifferent civil considering the Cuntry from whence they came; they were under the command of Lockhert once Governor of Dunkirke, the first time

43 Manningtree.

that I ever heard the Scotch came peaceably into England. Here is a large market place and an old Towne-Hall.

On the 23rd about one of the clocke we departed from Ipswich and wrodd along the county of Suffolk (being for the most part barren, and sandy) till we came to Beckles,[44] being thirty miles compleate; nothing but inconsiderable villages in the way, excepting some faire seats with parks, as that belonging to Sir John Rouse. The towne is small scituate upon the River Waveney which divides the counties of Norfolk and Suffolk for a greate way together. Here is a spatious church and tower erected for the most part at the charge of the Reades of Weston Hall which seate is within a mile of the towne. This place labor'd under the like oppression with the former, but with a ruder sort of ruffins cal'd Dragoons: insomuch that we found it difficult to obtaine any lodging. 200 of them were quarter'd upon this poore place, and had runn 300£ into the peoples debts; and if they demanded any thing they would fopp 'um off with this answere that they had moneys ready at London, but they could not gett Bills of retourn yet. These are the frutes of Kingly Goverment.

Yarmouth

ON THE 24TH of this Instant we wrode over Waveney and so came into Norfolk, this part of the cuntry is low and sandy and for the most part floated; we travel'd through a litle island cal'd Loving-Land;[45] by noone we arrived at Yarmouth a towne famous throughout Europe for a herring trade. The antient name was Gariamonum frome the River Garienis now Yere and so Yeremouth.[46] The Key is the most spatious that I have seene being in most places 20 yards over, and so continuing along the towne: ships of 200 tunn may easily ly before it. The buildings are faire and beautifull lying in two lines which make a streete betwixt about a mile and a half in length. On the other side is a faire wide space betweene the towne and the wall which is the market-place. Here is a litle fortification erected by our late Commonwealth 2 or 3 small forts in one whereof lying upon the sea is a battery of iron gunns. The cross lanes from the Key are so narrow that they are forc't to use cargo's for their goods like wheele-barrows drawne with one horse the driver standing upon it: and so whirring along, just as they describe the fighting of the Antient Brittains. The people obliging, and not like the bores of Harwich. We had here good provision, and good wine. We enter'd into a large ample church full of seates and galleries with a young library but nothing else observable. The

44 Beccles.
45 Lothingland.
46 The River Bure flows through Yarmouth.

Goverment is by Bayliffs 24 Aldermen and a Councel of 40. We went off from hence about 6 in the evening, and wrode through a sandy bottom, and by chance mett with a good Guide who about 11 of the clock that night brought us to Norwich.

Norwich

A T NORWICH WE remain'd all day being Sunday the 25th. The cuntry round about the towne is a fruitfull valley. It is water'd with the river Hierus[47] which brings up boats into the hart of the towne in some places. It is closed with a large flint wall (excepting on the river side) for allmost five miles in compass with watch towers all along at convenient distances. The streets are large, the houses for the most part of an antient building. A large market-place adorn'd with crosses and conducts [?conduits]. An old ruinous castle (that serves for the county gaole) with the deepest trench that ever I beheld. The bridge leading to the castle over the trench ha's a verry wide arch. The gate before you come to't shows a mighty ruine, 'twas blowne up in the time of Ketts Rebellion for feare he should take possession of it and so annoy the citty. At the entring into the towne they show'd a decayed building cal'd Ketts Fort where he first show'd himself. Here is an old brick being the pallace of the Duke of Norfolke with the motto over the gate, *Virtus sola invicta*, a faire garden belonging to it but remote from the house. Here are variety of goodly churches with lofty towers flay'd with flint; about 35 parishes; on one of the towers upon a sundiall was the inscription *Labilis Hora fugit*. The Cathedral is a large building with divers carv'd columns, the rooff over the quire is magnificent richly guilded, and illustrated with the stories of the Old Testament in painting. The people for the most part obliging and curteous. Here is the most noted manufacture of stuffs in all our Island. Our entertainment was here good and reasonable but ill attendance; so from hence early the nex(t) morning we departed.

Thetford

O N THE 26 we travel'd through Norfolk in a champaign cuntry till we came to Thetford an antient towne demollisht by the Danes standing partly in both counties Suffolk and Norfolk, a litle river dividing it, which I conceive to bee part of Waveney. Here we view'd the vast ruines of a religious house destroy'd in the raigne of Henry 8 and a strange Roman fort, cast up with earth and inviron'd with 3 trenches. Here they told of some villages neere the place that were much infested with the driving of sands when the wind sate

47 The river Yare is navigable, and the Wensum, Tud and Tas also flow through Norwich.

that way insomuch that some of them had been overwhelm'd by it; we dined here and went onward to St Edmunds Bury that night. The Romans stiled it Sitomagus and was afterwards the seate of the king of the East Angles.

We lay at the *Three Kings* in St Edmunds Bury the night and the next morning being the 27th walk't about the towne but we found it not to answere the character that had been given of it; it ha's been encompass't with a wall the gates are yet remaining. Neere the monastery the buildings are faire, the streets wide and hansome. The monastery was first founded by Canute in honor of King Edmund who was slaine there, and so denominated the place; there is remaining to this day a most spatious court of ruin'd building, adjoining to it is a churchyard with 2 beautifull churches the fairest of whch is dedicated to St James in which is the tomb of St Edmund the Martyr'd king and another for the wife of Charles Brandon: both remov'd out of the Abby upon the demollishing. The towne is pretty large, and being upon a moderate rise somwhat scanty which is all that we could observe in it.

St Edmunds Berry

O N THE 27TH in the morning we left St Edmunds Bury we wrode over the Downs, and pass't over a place vulgarly cal'd the Devils Ditch being (indeede) a fence made by the East Angles against the Mercians. Here after dinner we went to see the Kings Hunting House: but we could only obtaine a sight of the Duke of Buckinghams apartment, which was very noble, in his lodging chamber in an alcove stood the brave bed presented him by the king of France in his embassy, a rich looking glass, the roome was hung with blew damask strain'd. In the next roome we saw a device in the sealing with pullies which we conceiv'd a structure for letting down of mistresses(?). From here we departed to the towne of Cambridge.

Cambridge

B Y NIGHT WE reach't Cambridge and remain'd there all the 28th and 29th searching the manuscripts of the publick Library, and observing the medalls amongst many things in Jesus College Chappel, which was antiently the place of devotion for a nunnery, on a tombstone in old characters was this epitaph *Moribus ornata jacet hic Bona Burta Rosata.*

On the 30th at night we lodge'd at the *RaineDeere* in Bishop Stafford[48] a speciall spunging house. We saw here a large spatious parish church.

On the 31 we retourn'd for the Citty of London.

---

48 Bishops Stortford.

4
A JOURNEY TO PARIS

A voyage taken on the 7th of August 1673.

O N THE 9TH of this Instant about 4 of the clock in the morning we sett saile in the pacquet boate having had a pretty quick passage; but the tide having left us when we came into the harbour, we were forc't to make ashore in a long-boate; but the unskillfull seamen runne us in with much danger, so that had not some mercenary fellows come in timely who waded into the sea, and took us out upon their shoulders we might have been oversett, or washt overboard. We walk't allmost a mile upon the sand, ferried over a small water and so enter'd the towne of Calais. Here we visited the Minims which are friars of the order of St Francis, and on the Sunday being the 10th saw the towne-bred offer'd at the high altar. It was brought in on a beare upon the shoulders of 2 virgins dresst alike in a livery, being consecrated and sprinkled with holy water, twas afterwards distributed amongst severall persons. At the end of the service the Governour the Count de Sharroe with the rest of the gentry follow'd the priest (with their banners) in a solemne procession about the church. From hence in the evening we were carried in the Duke of Monmouths coach to Gaen[49] a poore thatch't ville having a small fort upon a hill, this towne has been fir'd twice, or thrice by the Spanniard and looks verry despicable.

The cuntry here about is cal'd the *paie reconque*. We pass't through Swoft?[50] a poore village lying upon the frontiers dividing the French and the Spaniard. We from hence enter'd Flanders in our waggon, and by noone came to St Omers, a strong fortified large towne belonging to the Spaniard. We pass't over 4 draw-bridges at the entrance. The Governour ha's here a large house about the midle of the towne; the bores were here diligently bringing in their goods for protection, a great body of the prince of Condies Horse approaching neere the place. We view'd the church of St Audomar and the Jesuites College, and that evening went away for Heir another towne in Flanders in the Spannish

49 Guines (Guisnes) in Pas-de-Calais.
50 'Swoft' not identified; St Omer; Aire-sur-la-Lys.

Subjection, 'tis well fortified 3 draw bridges at the entrance. We had but ordinary entertainment here at a great fatt Flemmings. The next morning we went to see a small house of the poore English Clares, the Lady Abbess was named Holford, 4 Franciscan friers lodg'd in the same house; wee discourst with one of them who inveighed much against the tyrannicall proceedings of the king of France.

This being the 12th we went away and enter'd the province of Artois, and so came to Lilier;[51] here we saw a regiment of horse belonging to the prince of

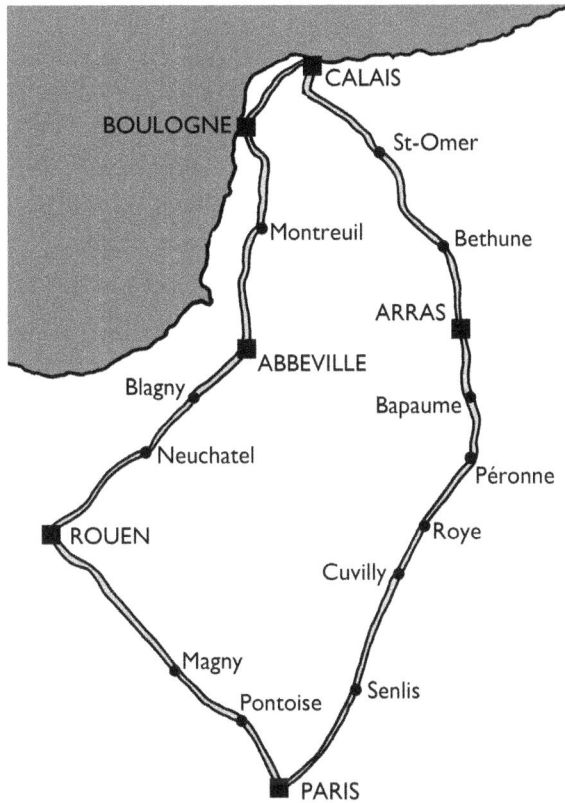

Condies army under the command of the Duke of Mevel, for the most part they appeard pretty well. We went afterwards to Bethune a towne in Artois where we were show'd the church of St Bartholomew, and severall reliques in it, as a golden cross with a thorn and a holy naile set in it. The right arm of St Bartholomew the Apostle preserv'd in a silver chest, being a present from one of the kings of Hungary, this was flec'd [?] when the Goodman suffer'd martyrdome. We were conducted afterwards to the chappel of the Confreres where they show'd us a bone of St Elois arm sett in a case of silver. I had allmost forgot that at St Bartholomews church where we saw the history of our Saviour praying in the Garden, lively represented in statuary worke; the steeple guilded and adorned with flower d'ly's. We departed hence and came that night to Arrhas, a large populous towne and the metropolis of Artois, here they were mightily fortifying. Here they show'd us the tower of La Santa Chandele which was built in the forme of a taper spiring up in flame in which was kept a ridiculous miracle,

51 Lillers? Arras; La Sainte-Chandelle.

likewise the great Abby of Senvau[52] with the House of the Recolets and a large beautifull church of Nostredame, the tower whereof we ascended to view the towne. 'tis an episcopall see. The Market show'd us great plenty of fish. Here was a large old building erected by Count Egmond and likewise a faire old structure inhabited by the Governour whome they stiled Duke d'Monpizat.

We departed hence on the 13th Instant and took our journey to Vaponne[53] on the confines of Artois, the king was repairing the fortifications here, about 900 men in garrison, whereof 300 were Switzes; all along this province we came through a delightfull champaigne. We dined here and lodg'd that night at Peronne a towne in Picardy. As we passt betweene these townes we came by 2 Abbies most delightfully seated; they were fortifying this place allso so that I find the king values noe expences. The next day being the 14th Instant and St Bartholomews day, we heard the friers chant High Mass, and so took our journey to Rey[54] where we din'd. Coming into this towne we found the women sitting out in the streets and playing at dice for diversion being holyday. By the way we founded our selves much infested with the souldiers companions which is common to travellers in France, but we found the cause proceeded from our driver who us'd to lodge in the waggon and so left his Creepers behind him.

We sett forward to Queville,[55] and by the way saw a fair house of the Marchie d'Sancors Grand Avener to the king, and was then attending on him at the Champaign at Nancy in Lorrain, here was a spatious stable and in it severall English horse. We lodg'd at this meane village in a poore Caberet, and the next morning being the 15th took our journey towards Gourney[56] where we mett with nothing but an old seat castle-building and a wellwoodded large parke. We pass't along the Val d'ore the cuntry was sandy but not so fruitfull as Artois, here we found the cuntry more sensibly hott than in England. We were like to have been retarded in our journey by an order of the kings for stopping of vagrant souldiers from the camp, had we not produc'd our letters, and Bills of Exchange for Paris which clear'd the matter and so by the evening we arriv'd at Senlis, which is pretty large but the works for the most part demollisht. We came hither on a holyday, they were then entertaining their Governor who was the Marchee de St Simon. Comming hither we saw the peasant reaping of oates instead of mowing of them as we doe.

52 Saint-Vaast?

53 Bapaum; Peronne.

54 Roye.

55 Cuvilly. Walker was following close to the present A1 route to Paris.

56 Gourney not identified; Senlis.

On the 16 Instant we left this place and so came [to] Chapelle,[57] thence to Parisee, the way sett with rows of trees for the most part, but the soile not so good as before. The cuntry lay thick with small townes. We went over part of the Forrest of Countslan and so upon a causey to Paris. We pass't by the towne of Monmartir, which is inhabited by bakers and that night arrived at this great citty. We took up our lodging in the Rue d'Money which is close by the Mint. Sunday the 17 we went to the church of St German which is the parish church to the Lover,[58] the roofe guilded with flower d'lis'es. We went afterwards to the church of Nostredame being the feast of our Lady and heard High-Mass celebrated with solemne processions, the Arch-bishop of Paris in his miter, and pontificalibus blessing the people, and acting a great deale of ridiculous legerdemaine. At the entrance into the church one of the columes that supported the 2 towers was carv'd into the figure of St Christopher standing upon a rock allmost in proportion like the romantick Pantagruel mention'd by Rablais. Going up to the Quier on the right hand stands the statue of Philip the August on horseback, upon the obtaining of some victory he vow'd to offer up his horse to the Holy Virgin, which he did accordingly at the high altar, and afterwards erected this in commemoration of the fact. The church was hung about with ensignes and colors most of them trophies taken from the Dutch in severall skirmishes with this motto upon many of them *Pro Focis et Aris*.

The Loaver which is the Kings Pallace is a stately building lying along the river, 'tis design'd to bee built in a vast quadrangle, but onely 2 sides yet erected, that along the river side was erected by Henry 4 that on Thouleries[59] or Garden was compiled by this king all of stone, he designes to pull downe above 1000 houses to inlarge it. The gallery is 600 yards in length, but the breadth and height no way proportionable to it, it was then unfinisht; underneath is a stable capacious enough to contain 240 horse affording each a particular stand. In the outer court of the pallace stands the stable of the Mannage horses which were about 60 in number, the custome is here to pull of your glove upon entring least the groomes demand a forfeiture. The king traines up all his pages to horsemanship, they constantly ride every morning, fence, and are instructed in the mathematicks and so are fitted for his warrs.

The pallace is richly guilded, the stately roome of Audience sett with costly cabinets, a faire chimney piece one which was the pourtraiet of the king of France riding into Danekirke, an angel pouring out of money at his comming into the towne. But that which surpassed all was the glory of the

---

57 Chapelle? Montmartre.

58 Louvre, spelled Lover or Loaver throughout the next pages.

59 Tuileries, also spelled 'Touleries'.

Theater so rich a roofe and such variety of machines with such exquisite painting that it exceeded the glory of the Banqueting House at Whitehall. In some of the roomes were the models of his frontiere townes sett upon tablets exactly demonstrating their fortifications and the ground how they lay. The heads of Alexander and Homer and some other antiquities; great heapes of marble for the beautifying of it, and what was most admired, 2 stones 18 yard long apiece, and 4 broade which were brought there to make the capitall of an arch.

The Touleries is a large delightfull garden with jettos playing, and a greene Theater set with cypresses for acting in the heate of summer; at the farther end are 2 mounts for prospect and a way leading to Versailes, and so I conclude my view of the Lover.

Hospitalls

WE WENT AFTERWARDS to see the the (sic) Hostel d'Dieu, an hospitall large enough to containe 10 or 12000 people standing hard by the Church of Nostredame. From hence to the Mason d' la Charity not neere so large as the former, but much cleanlier and neater, this was most for weake sick men, the beds all of white dimity verry neate 2 rows along the cloyster containing about 100 in a side, the laye nunns, or sisters tending of them, and preparing necessaries, litle roomes on the sides for removing of such as grew more languishing and weake that they may end their dayes the quieter, the friers allso applying their spirituall comfort.

Palais Royall

WE COME NOW to the Palais Royall a fair large structure erected by Cardinal Richlieu at the time that he was Admirall of France so that the building is carv'd with anchors cables and the ends of ships on the outside. Upon his death it came to the Crowne and is since made the pallace for Monseur and Madame; the roomes are extreamly guilded and carv'd here. The Monseurs apartment was verry magnificent, his Roome of Audience was sett with cabinets, a long gallery with the pictures of antient heroick monseurs as the Duke of Espernon Momerancy p t: the heads of the Cæsars, Petrarch and some of the Italian poets. Severall litle figures of copper cast from the Roman models of the fight betweene a lyon and a horse, a lyon and a bull reported to bee taken out of the old Duke of Buckinghams closet who was stab'd by Felton. The heads of some of the Greeke deities. In his lodging chamber stood a great plate looking-glass, table, and stands of the same with silver baskets of philigren worke sett upon them which they say cost 200 000 crownes. A rich bed, and bedsted all ebony and plated with silver the sprigs on top of the same, variety of mirrors of ebony plated. Rare painting, among which was a verry amorous picture of a young lady that attended Madamaselle d'Orleans the Monseurs first Lady, with verry light haire curl'd and plentifully flowing about her brests and shoulders. In his closset were a multitude of toyes, litle pictures with silver frames, and litle silver cabinets. Another cabinet all of christall which was in the gallery.

The Duchesses apartment was carv'd and guilded in like manner for the most part, her bed and chamber furnisht with China silkes, the railes of the alcove all massie silver, the furniture of the chimney of the same, 2 faire christall branches for candles hanging downe from the roofe of the chamber. I omitted one thing observable which is the picture of Maria d' Medici riding a hunting with a train of young ladies on horseback, one of them falling off discovers a pleasing nakedness. This was the place allotted for the reception of our exiled king, and duke at Paris.

Here it may not bee insignificant to give a briefe character of the Monseur, who in the opinion of all people is a verry weake person, altogether uncapable of transacting any publick affaires insomuch as the king keepes him upon a stipend or annuall, not allowing him to claime anything as his owne, and did frequently complain to him of the contempts and abuses put upon him by his first Lady.

College of painters

WE ENTER'D HERE first into a wide court sett about with pictures expos'd to publick view, in the midst upon a pedestall we saw another brass horse with the effigies of the present king, severall draughts above stairs likewise with the skeletons of men and women. Passing hither I remember my companion Tasburgh mett with Father Goff whome I understood to bee a great mannager of the Duke of Monmouth by which we may know how he stands inclin'd, and this being the 18th in the evening we saw fireworks perform'd by the Augustine friers being their festivall.

St Innocents Church

THIS IS A dark building with a cloyster about it much like that at Suttons Hospitall in which are severall small shops. It was founded by one Nicholas Flemming a scrivener, or notary in this citty who (because of his great wealth) was supposed to have found out the philosophers stone; the heate of the earth here is such that if a corps bee inter'd it consumes it in the space of 24 houres. Here were vast heapes of bones lying in galleries over the arch of the cloyster.

Val d' Grace

FROM THENCE WE came to this beautifull chappel founded by Anne of Austria late Queene Mother of France, a verry stately building to which is added a faire nunnery. Over the portall at the entrance was this inscription *Jesu nascenti virginiq. matri*. At the upper end within stood a glorious altar over it an arch richly guilded supported by 6 wreath'd marble columnes, above that a cupola in which paradise was painted and in it the Queene in a gowne studded with flower d' L'ys's.

Palais

NOW WE CAME to the Palais del Isle which is in the nature of our Exchange, a faire ascent of stone steps, but the place not so beautifull, their shops full of toies, and knick-knacks, by it a neate chappel with painted windows, this was antiently a pallace for their kings. Here is a large hall with shops as that at Westminster, here there parlement is held their Courts of Judicature, and the severall offices belonging to their Mercenary Advocates, who swarm here more abundantly than in England, corruption being here an avow'd thing, for they all buy their places of the king, and must of course sell justice or injustice by retaile to the people to make up themselves again. No trials by juries here the Judge examines every criminall privately in his closet, and so ha's his women, or Baude of Justice, that goes privately and proposes a price of ease, or redemption to the malefactor, and this is the thing our courtiers labor to bring us too in England.

Circle Royall

HERE WE BEHELD a pretty toy, which was the figures of the kings, queens and principall nobility of both courts, made in wax in full proportion to the life in their habit a la mode. My Lord Arlington was verry lively represented with the patch on his nose, and the Countess of Northumberland made much more lovely than the Duchess of Clevelande the rest not so well in all about 3 or 4 and twenty in number. The Court of France was neere twice as many among which were La Valier and Montispan, the first with 2 children by her begotten by the king, the other was made standing, so that I find those things that are reckon'd vices, and crimes in the inferior sort of men, are the glories and triumphs of haughty monarchs. On the side of the French Court without the raile stood the head of Oliver Cromwell with a flaming countenance and stern look donne to the brest in the manner of the Cesars, this was poorly given by our king out of his owne closset to the French-man that was the framer of these images. Over the doore at the entrance of the house stood the head of Scarramuccio that was invited over to show tricks and cheate the gentry at York-House.

Palais d' Luxemburgh[60]

THIS BELONGS TO two sisters, who are of the blood, being daughters to the old Duke of Orleans uncle to the king, the one is the Duchess of Monpensier, the other the Duchess of Guise, the first an antient maide, the other a widdow who ha's one only child who is stil'd Duke of Alauson. The king keepes a strict eye over them, in hopes their revenue which is verry great may revert to the Crowne.

This pallace is a noble pile of building, a large quadrangle in the midle, on the farther side a fair garden in which the gentry for their recreation walk as we do in Grays Inne. By the help of an Irish sæcular priest we saw the Duchess of Guise and her rich apartment; in her Chamber were many curious pictures of the present Duke of Tuscany and his Lady, the Duke of Savoy, and an excelent piece of the king, the head of Maria d' Medici in white marble with a great ruffe. The next day we obtain'd the favour of seeing the gallery of Reuben here, counted one of the greatest curiosities in Europe, the roof extreamly beautified with guilding and painting. All the sides of the gallery were illustrated with the history of Maria d' Medici (design'd and drawne by the famous painter Reuben) from her cradle to her tombe, which was so hansomly contriv'd you would have deem'd her the most virtuous woman in her time, the Fates and the Graces being brought to direct most part of her Life.

The House of the Astrologers

THIS WAS ERECTED at the charge of the king with a pension for the support of such a number of men who are to profess this science. This was a faire stone building with a speculatorie tower on top, but not neere finished while we were there. Here we saw the designe of a much larger telescope than that in St James's park, the whispering roome made all about with angles which conveyed the sound readier than that at Glocester, 2 outaxonstons or speaking trumpets the invention of Sir Samuel Moreland and presented by him to this king well guilded with inscriptions of latine verses.

Pont Neuf

OF ALL THE parts about the citty of Paris this is certainly the most delightfull, the Lover running all on one side the river and the College

60 Luxembourg.

of the Quator Nations[61] on the other, which was founded by the Cardinal
Junius Muzarinus and is a verry stately building with fair guilt cupoli on top.
The river is adorn'd with many beautifull structures for a mile on each side
being from Pont Rouge to Pont a Nostredame. But the most magnificent is
the midle bridge cal'd Pont Neuf being the maine passage betwixt the citty
and the fauxburge or suburbs; the foot way is rais'd high on each side so that
the coaches and carts goe a matter of 4 or 5 foot below you without any
incumbrance to passengers. Upon the comming out of the citty on the right
hand is a waterhouse, the water flowing off of a sheete of copper into a cistern,
wherein are the figures of our Saviour and the Samaritan woman as if they were
discoursing at the fountain. About the midle is the effigies of Henry 4 in brass
riding on horseback of double proportion standing upon a high pedestall, and
looking towards the bridge of Nostredame. The pedestall bares this inscription.

Quisquis hæc legis, ita legito uti optimo principi precaberis exercitum fortem,
populum fidelem, imperium securum et annos de nostris. B. B. F.

Arcule[62]

O N SUNDAY IN the afternoone we took coach and went to see this
worke standing about a league from the citty. It is an aquæduct built by
Cardinal Richleu for the supply of Paris. It is built upon twenty large arches at
least, and rising about 40 foot high, on top of which (the water comming out
of the hills) runns violently along a small channel of stone, and so descends
into pipes for the citty. There is belonging to it a pleasant summer-house with
hanging gardens on the side of the hill. As we ascended the steps to the house
we were entertained with a curious prospect (through a roome of pictures)
into an arch of greene which seem'd as if painted, but passing into it we found
it an antient decaying arbor. The place was wonderfully contriv'd for delight
and retirement, variety of grots and waterworks, the hills hanging over and
obscuring the walkes; the water thrilling about and doubtless would afford
extreame satisfaction were it not now neglected and growne ruinous.

Palais Mazarine

T HIS PALLACE WAS built by the Cardinal of that name and given in
marriage to the Duke d' Mazarine who married his neece, but she proving
loose and wanton ha's occasion'd a separation betweene 'um. Here you may

61 Collège des Quatre-Nations also known as the Collège Mazarin after its founder,
    was one of the colleges of the historic University of Paris.
62 Arcueil.

plainly see the Cardinal spar'd no cost in getting rarities from all parts of the world. It is not verry large but the inside wonderfull rich and stately. At our first entrance we saw severall curiosities drawn by the hand of Titian all naked, but the Duke being priest ridden was perswaded to cause some painters of Paris to draw a vaile over the members (which ha's much prejudic't the worke) they suggesting that this might have occasion'd his Lady to play the wanton. Here we saw a draught of our aged English par [?] and an old piece of that most ingenious Rablais the phisitian. In another roome we were entertain'd with some African rarities as the effigies of the goddess of Nature giving suck to an infant, the statue of the goddess Ceres of a kind of yellow marble. We saw a curious pourtraiture of nymphs and satyrs drawne with a pen at large in black and white much exceeding that of King David at Lackham, it was cover'd over with 2 large leafs of brass in a guilded frame. We saw severall earthen dishes painted by the famous Italian Raphael. The picture of this Raphael (being a smirking young fellow) drawne by his owne hand. Michael Angelo's mother with an old wrinkled face suppos'd to bee drawne by the sonne. The head of a Bashaw drawn by a verry exact Dutch hand, the Roman Lucrece stabbing of her self, two or three severall pieces of the Cardinal drawne at length. The heads of Marcus Aurelius the Emperor and his wife carv'd upon an old stone tablet a true Roman worke.

We saw 2 brass-heads growne black with time one of Seneca the tragedian the other of Cicero the orator. The first was large brow'd and of a stern look, the other was thinner favor'd, thinn lips and a wart upon the left side of his face. The variety of delicate pictures besides was all-most infinite, some wrote in silks some wove and some in mosaick work.

After this wonderfull variety we enter'd into a long gallery adorn'd with many antique figures sett in guilded neeches. Over the dores at each end were the heads of Pompey and Cesar, the statue of the god Mercury with the wings in's hat; severall of the Roman emperors at large. The heads of the 12 Cesars in copper obducted with marble mantles exact copies from those at Rome, and of great proportion. Cleopatra with her hands folded over her head in a mournfull posture. Hercules in a vast gigantick figure with his club in his right hand and the spoyles of a lyon throwne over his left arm. Another figure of his dying upon Mount Oetæ proportion'd to admiration. Two tombstones brought from Rome, carv'd with horses and men in flight which we imagined to bee the victories of some inter'd emperors. Many rare cabinets; on the top of one of them was a litle figure of Pompey on horseback guilded. On the frontispiece were severall fair stones allmost square nigh 2 inches over, representing the lapis lazuli with many other colors brought from Rome and taken out of Nero's bath there. This

Cardinal bought as many of them as cost him 30,000 livers and had them sett in 2 dressing tables to bee presented to the Queene Mother with home he was supposed to have an intimate familiarity by their steering the French affairs.

In the same gallery we saw diverse Roman urns of white marble, others of porphiry and of different shapes some in the manner of our earthen pots that we bake in sloaping less and less towards the bottom, others much larger in the manner of our big-bellyd pipkins, with covers of the same. Tis verry remarkable that they tell you that this art of working in porphiry is now generally losst in Italy, for it is so solid that it sparkles in the face of the artificer and know no meanes to prevent the inconveniency of it. In a roome below stairs we saw a paire of antique andirons made at Rome which represented the Thunderer and's wife, one riding on an eagle with thunder in his hand, the other with a scepter riding on her peacock; each bird had 6 giants for a pedestall; these were of copper, the like made in silver, and standing in the roome where the silver table was which I mention'd before. In the roome without the gallery stood the figure of Mark Anthony on horsback; the Duke caus'd most of the antient statues to have their members veil'd over with playster of paris, but it ha's not donne so much injury as that to the paintings because this may bee taken off again

St Germans

AUGUST THE 27TH we took coach and went a way for St Germans being an antient castle building of brick flag'd with stone, with a deepe dry graft about it. The chiefest rarity here was the kings apartment, the flores all delicately inlaide in severall works with crowns flower d'lis's and his proud motto *nec pluribus impar*. In the neeches of the roome many silver figures upon broade pedestalls of the same all massie. His bedchamber in like manner inlaide all about in which stood the richest bed that ever I saw, the counterpan, and curtaines all wove of gold and silver as if one entire piece of lace, with a rich fringe about it, the bedsted all of massie silver in an alcove with a raile of the same before it. At the head of the bedsted were mirrors set in frame of silver supported by cupids of the same. In the midle of the tester likewise a circle of mirrors, which might represent the various postures that lovers use; we were told this was the place where he did use to recreate himselfe with Montispan. From hence we were conveyed through a narrow passage into a round place cal'd his Cabinet or dressing rome, this was sett with glasses all from top to bottom, and stripes of lapis lazuli betweene the guilded frames. Here was sett a fountain of silver and many figures of the same. Along the sides of this apartment went a Terra's Walk guarded with guilded batlements from whence you might take a prospect of the garden and woods.

The Queens apartment was inferior to this, only a bed of greene velvet lin'd with cloth of gold a counterpane of the same, imbroidered hangings and some pictures of the kings of Spaine. Here in a large old rome we were show'd how the Douphin was instructed in military discipline with leaden figures of horse and foot and artillery, together with all sorts of maps for his instructions both in antient and modern geography. The garden here afforded no great matter of rarity. In it was a neate small house belonging to Monseur Colebert who has gott the ascendant allmost as much as our Chancelor had. Here was a litle open guilded chariot made like those triumphall at Rome for the diverting of his daughter begott on Montispan, being to bee drawne about by 6 dogs, a litle example of the impertinencie of monarchs. We left this place and in the evening went to Mazons in the coach.

Mazon's.

THIS IS A faire seate built of freestone lying upon the side of the River Seyne, belonging to Monseur Longuele president of the parlament at Paris; the house is of the modern Italian model, wrather exquisitely neat than rich. The hall was pav'd with marble affording a delicat prospect. At the entrance large folding dores of carv'd iron, the romes lofty and well-proportion'd; in one of them stood a black-velvet-bed of the highest imbroidery that ever I saw, with furniture of the same. The cabinet here was very pretty being inlaide with cedar in the shape of birds. The garden adorn'd with knots and orange trees, lying along upon the side of the river. The stables mighty commodious, over the midle was a large cupola under which they wrode the Mannage, it contain'd about 80 horse in all. On the right side was a grott of shells and artificiall rocks, the water running into a large cistern of stone, out of which the horses dranke, and were at the same time washt with severall spouts and jetto's of water. We left this place and ferried twice over the Seyne passing through variety of vinyards and so came back the night to Paris.

The English Benedictines, and Nunnery of Carmelites the next day

THE BENEDICTINES WERE a black habit as the Augustines, they had a small House here and were about twenty in number, one of them sate and discourst with us about an hour. In the rome where we were they had hung up the heads of severall abots that had suffer'd martyrdome as (they call it) under Henry 8. From hence we went to the rich endow'd nunnery of the Carmelites. It was begunne by that notorious Maria d' Medici; here we beheld a verry glorious chappel. On the top of the gallery comming in stood the effigies of Michael the Archangel carv'd in marble triumphing over Satan with a broad sword in his hand, and Satan plac't under his feet just as if he were rolling off of the batlement.

Arc d' triumph

THIS IS A piece of vanity standing a litle without the towne, erected only for a model of approbation, the king intending to take downe this again and erect one intirely of marble all in Corinthian worke. Betweene the columnes in large circles are carv'd the conquer'd cities in Flanders. On the top now of stone is intended to bee erected a copper horse of vast proportion, with the figure of the king richly guilded. This verry model (which is but upon likeing) stood the king in 30000£ sterling. The way all on this side the citty was adorn'd with rows of trees too like a garden.

Icy[63]

SUNDAY BEING THE 30th we went to Icy about a league from Paris where we saw a large garden on the side of a hill with solitary walks, and jetto's, the ground gently descending towards the River Seyne; but now going to decay. Twa's belonging to Monseur Sabonier Chancelor of France but now a declin'd statesman and fallen under a cloude.[64]

Bibliothec-Royall

IN THIS WAS severall square roomes full of books many printed at the king's expence which were all bound in red-leather with large filletings of gold which they call the Lover print, and binding. For particulars here were twelve folios of an herball most naturally described in colors.. Books of all sorts of fish painted to the life. Books of the anatomy of most sorts of beasts. Manuscripts both Greeke and Latine, Arabick, and Persiack verry antient and curiously color'd; the letters of many of the Kings, and Queens of France, as of Lewis the 13th, Maria de Medici, and other great persons of the Court. A folio of this kings exercizes when he was a boy. Severall cabinets full of Roman coines. Many Egyptian gods made of earth. Litle Egyptian idolls of wood painted standing upon pedestalls of the same, to bee sett at the head of the deceased as tutelar gods. In the first roome we came in lay a large Egyptian mummy in a coffin, or case of wood proportion'd to the shape of the body, wrapt up in ser-cloth with perfum'd gumms, the covering of the face and head guilded, upon the brest a label in hieroglyphicks. Isis and her sonne Osiris in her arms in brass. Another

63 Issy-les-Moulineaux?
64 Pierre Séguier?

antient figure of Isis in blackstone with hieroglyphicks. Below in a rome where used to bee a consultation of phisitians stood a large burning sphere which in a short time would melt iron at 10 foot distance. It was compos'd at Lyons of mettall like burnisht steele, and cost 7000 livers. On the other side of this we saw the Kings Laboratory.

Versailes[65]

WEE TOOK COACH at Paris and passt through St Clou a towne seated on the side of a hill, containing a fair seat belonging to the Monseur, at the foot runns the River Seyne, and so we went to the beauteous pallace of Versailes being 6 league from Paris. This was formerly but a small hunting-house for the king to lodge in after his recreations, but is now the most glorious structure of Europe, a large court opening with iron gates at the entrance, at the upper end a jetto in the middle of a marble pavement, and 2 great scollopt basons of white marble, all the balconies carv'd and richly guilded, the spouts guilded, and painted, the 2 wings of the building batlemented at each end, and sett with large figures, the kitchin and other offices sett apart from the great building. The roomes were not quite finisht within dores, but enough to declare his magnificent intentions, for most of them for a yard deepe were inlaide upon the walls with various color'd marble, the sides of the windows so too with large folding dores of broad christall glass.

At the front of the house towards the great garden, stands a peazo with Corinthian columns, batlemented on top, with a large marble walk and a jetto in the midle, the kings lodgings opening into it. In the queens apartment we saw a cabinet finely inlaide with ivory, an alcove striped downe with broad mirrors. In the bilyard roome was the kings-picture drawne at length in armor (according to the antient Roman manner) pointing to a towne upon a hill as if he design'd to attack it. At the upper end of the rome hung the pourtraiture of Madam Montispan lying carelessly upon a palat, a quiver hanging upon her right arm, and diverse cupids comming to steale arrows out of it. Her breasts were naked her feet in sandalls brac't about with silk strings. Her leggs appearing naked up to the risings of her calves, affording great delight to the beholder. From hence we enter'd into the large garden and being upon a holy-day we had the opportunity of seeing all the waterworks play, the Douphin and Madam comming out to the passtime. Here we saw the king had been at vast charges to bring water at a long distance to supply this place, being seated upon a dry sandy hill, so that the water is forc't up by windmills and horses to bee conveyed into all parts of the garden.

65 Versailles; Saint-Cloud.

From a terra's we descended the wide steps and so came to the waterworks, the division betweene sett with statues, and flower-pots. The first was severall copper froggs vomiting of water; the next as many tortoises doing the like, then the guilded crowne overflowing, and empting it self into a bason; 2 rows of stands guilded the water gently falling into sheetes. From hence we came downe to a large waterworke with severall dolphins guilded and a whale in the midle spouting up water a vast height, which by the reflection of the sunne represented a rainbow. From hence we went into a fair square in which stood 2 large oval tables of marble, upon the midle of these stood 2 baskets of flowers made of copper guilded and finely painted issuing out with water, on the sides were basons and gores [slits?] and such like that did the same; in the midle was a square pond at each corner a great guilded swan spouting of water, at the sides severall flaggs seem'd to grow which were made of tin and painted green. In the midst stood a tree upon a litle island, every branch spouting out severall streames of water, and so did the flaggs. Then we came downe to the long walk, sett with pots painted in the manner of China work at the bottom, which cast out water and made an arch over our heads as we went along.

Hence we went to the green Theater set with cypresses the pit 'circl'd with enamel'd shells the water gently drilling upon them. Above this were three walks all sett with such painted shells which plaid five rows of jetto's at a time, then made cross arches, then mett and broke into mists, refreshing the spectators as they sate at playes in the heat of summer. Then we went on to the long walk each side done with cross-bars in lattice work painted greene, the top sett with flower-pots color'd in the China manner, in all there were five walks of this worke which led us into a spatious circle of the same worke which they call the starr, adorn'd with guilded seats about. In the middle of this was a rock, out of which spouted vast quantities of water, to a mighty height, which descended in mists of cloudes. At the lower end was another waterworke Neptune and his sea-horses spouting and throwing of water. Next to this was cutt a fair canal about a mile in length, a walk of broadstone pav'd on the brim. Here he had a litle Man of Warr riding neately equipt, and severall sorts of pleasure boates, the canal towards the upper end divided into a cross: that on the right hand rann towards the Triano[66] his summer garden, that on the left to the Managery, his house for beasts and birds.

Triano

FROM THE RIGHT-HAND of the canal the water runns up to this Triano which is a garden compos'd for all sorts of delights, and pleasures. The

66 Trianon.

lower part of the garden which is the sanding place, abounds with oranges, lemons, citrons, pomegranads, and arbors of Spannish gessemin from one end to tother which are so fragrant that they allmost overcome the brain; below this was a verry shady wilderness. We ascended the steps to the upper part which was set with flowerpots, and flowers of all sorts of colours. At the upper end here stood the faire and most delightfull summer-houses, all the outside of the roof set with pots carv'd in Corinthian flourishes, all the dores and sides set with cristalls in frames of polisht iron, the flores all of painted tile, the inside done in works, and knots of blew, with large mirors set in frames of plaister of paris painted in the same manner; some romes full of your China pots, waterworks round about in the courts. In the corners of these romes were little retiring places hung about and furnisht with rich palats whereon the king us't to repose. All things here made to the utmost advantage for secret pleasures.

Managery[67]

H ERE WE SAW the elephant, the camels, the red-bull with the bunch upon his back, afterwards we saw the severall pens for foxes civet-cats rattones, porcupines and such like. In the same court was a pond containing various species of birds, next to this was the court of estriges, then the pelicans, then the mosels. At the upper end was a delicate dovery streaming with jetto's and currents of water, folding-gates of iron at the entrance of all these places. In the midle of the court comming in stood a fair building; underneath was a grotto above was a spatious roome hung with the pictures of all these beasts and fowle all in guilded frames. Rich palats for repose. Afterwards we went to the Orangery which was verry fragrant with this fruite and many other delicious sorts with abundance of large myrtles, with long vaults under-ground for the housing the fruite against cold weather.

I forgott to mention the grotto we saw comming into the great-garden wherein was the hydraulick and the branch't candlesticks the water comming downe in the stemms, and issuing out at each socket, besides many other rare contrivances.

Gobelins

T HIS WAS A large house like a college establisht for entertaining ingenious artificers for the king's peculiar use. In the first place we saw the painters. Here was a large piece that the Venetian Senate had presented to the king which was our Saviours washing his disciples feet which cost 50000 crowns. Another of the like extent of Alexanders Persian triumph. Another as large

67 Menagerie.

being Alexander and Ephestina [?] standing together, and the mother wife and daughter of Darius supplicating at his feete. This an ingraver was copying whereby I saw the curiosity of his art, and many others at work upon other designs. In another part we saw an Italian standing naked for a model representing the various lines and postures of the body, for the instruction of young men who were there ready to take scetches either with their pencills, or else to mould 'um up in clay.

We saw some working in various colord stones representing the Indian birds, some casting leaden Cupids for fountains, others making models of clay, some working figures of marble and stone others again carving in wood, and making cabinets and chimney pieces. Yet of all these things nothing so rare as the imbroidery and needle-work we saw, together with the great numbers of loomes weaving out the heroick acts of the king, such as his taking of Lisle, and Tourney, in which are his own pourtraits on horseback verry glorious wrought in gold. His League with the Switz, the models of his 12 great houses or palaces, all the borders deeply imbroider'd and well shadow'd, twas said hee intended his Dutch conquests might bee done in like manner, but the case is altered – they may bee spar'd now. All these artificers had their wages duly paid 'um every Saturday night, and the king made the benefit of their worke.

Petit Maso'ns[68]

THIS IS THEIR Bedlam, the French call it petit because every one of these mad-people of both sexes are kept in a litle house distinct one from t'other, some were singing masse, others inveighing against the king of France. We saw 'um receive their supper, which was a small piece of cheese, a lunchin of bred, and 2 pares to each of them, some call it Mazo'n d's Insensables. Here was litle else observable except a large chappel belonging to the palace.

Arsenall

HERE WE SAW the Kings Magazine stor'd up, several courts of building and a large garden in the midle, at the upper end stood the Bastile a verry old building erected (as they say) by the English. In the Arsenall were great preparations of salt-peter for gunpowder a vast armory of musquets, half pikes, double locks for the Guard d'Core, the models of all sorts of instruments for warr, as cannons morter-pieces and petars, then they show'd us a small gun of curious worke presented to the Douphin, which had 2 litle swords at the end thereof to make passes in case the shott miss't, many double barrels, battle

68 Petites Maisons.

axes. Back, brest, and head-piece. Ensignes taken from the Dutch, the trophies of his easy victories, some of them with the Belgian lyon and the sheafe of arrows with this motto *vis unita fortior*.

St Denys

WE TOOK COACH and went to this place, being about 2 league distant from Paris where stood the old church dedicated to this Saint and abundance of extream rich reliques kept in presses, and show'd gratis by a friar.

In the first place was the head of St Denys of massie gold sett with abundance of pretious stones. Then Charlemaign's Crowne and Sword, set with diamonds, rubies, and pearles. 2 gold cabinets besides of his giving and his royall robes, the head of the Maide of Orleans, her sword, with her picture over the press. An unicorns horn, a naile of the Cross. Judus his darke lanthorn that he came into to betray our Saviour withall, with many other knacks which the friar topt upon us as sacred reliques. From hence we descended to see the antient tombs of their kings. In a side chapel unfinisht stood a lofty tomb for Henry 2. Another for Katherine of Medici of white marble a great tomb with marble figures for Lewis the 12th. Below the steps on the side of the Quier was the Cardinall of Bourbon kneeling upon a high marble colume praying. Within the Quier towards the high altar was Lewis the 13th under a cannopy of velvet with escucheons, and paul over him, 2 lamps of filigreen silver burning at his head, it being the custom of France to keep their kings above ground so till the next king comes in his place by death. Here they show'd us a great font of porphyry made like a trough wherein King Dagobert was cristned. The church is of a plain old gothick building darkened with painted windows. The foundation [I think) is of lazie Augustine Friers.

On the 19th of 7br [September] I left Paris and went without any company but French in the Grand Curroch for Rhone. The first day we din'd at Pontois (which is just upon the borders of Normandy) a long scambling towne where was an English nunnery but I wanted time to see it. The day continued rainy, but by night we came and lodg'd at Manniæ a poore miserable village, where we had bad entertainment. The next morning by moonshine we mounted the caroch, and passt through St Clare another poore village, where were the ruines of an old castle. From hence to Frankaville, and so to Egni where we baited, the people appearing exceeding poore in all these parts of Normandy, poore litle boyes now and then mett us and runne by the coach, and sung psalmes, or some of the priests cant in hopes of an almes.

The cuntry for the most part stony, abounding much with corn, aples, and pares growing all along the wayes without any inclosure, but few vineyards in these parts. We afterwarde staid a litle at Floree where was a neat caberet at the foot of a hill, finely incompass't with meadows, woods and a river. We came that night late into Rhone, and were to go downe a steep hill in the dark to gett into the citty.

Rhone[69]

THIS CITTY IS of a great extent, and was formerly the seat of our Dukes of Normandy, but now much impoverisht by great taxes, and want of trade. It lies like a theater inviron'd with hills, only one opening into a spatious plain which extends which exends (sic) about 16 leagues upon a flat, the river Seyne circling the meadow about the towne, which makes it a peninsula as 'twere; from hence it runns to Haver d'Grace[70] where it empts it self into the sea. By this means it obtains all its commerce, so that with a spring tide ships may come here of 150 tunne, it flows 4 leagues above the towne, and yet it continues fresh water four leagues below it.

We saw the Burse where the merchants mett; on the right hand hung the pictures of many of their antient kings, all downe to Henry4 were stiled of the House of Valois, but from him to this time of the House of Bourbon. One of them Francis the 2nd of Valois was stil'd Roy d' France et Ecosse. Here in the market place of the D'voes, or Calf Market the Maide of Orleans was burn't by the English. In memory of her they have erected a fountain, on top under the capitall of an arch is her statue, but 'tis antiquated and worne by time. The great Church of Nostredame here, does much exceed that at Paris for largeness, all the upper part of the Quier rail'd in with brass barristers; on the right side of the wall of the Quier was the monument of that famous warrior John Duke of Bedford, being onely 2 black marble stones made up in the outside of the wall of the Quier. In this church was the largest organ that ever I saw, half on the one side of the body of the church and half on 'tother, the great pipes seeming to bee about 40 foot in heighth, and 2 yards about. The force of the aier was so strong in playing that they shook the windows in pieces whereupon they forc't to discontinue 'um and erect another paire.

We went to see the great bell which is cal'd George of Amboyes the, the Cardinall of this place[71] having bestow'd it upon the church; it weighs

69 Rouen.

70 Le Havre.

71 The bell was named after Georges d'Amboise; it cracked, and was melted down for cannon during the French Revolution.

40000lb and is 13 yards and three quarters in circumference, the dimensions of it are made out below at the entrance of the church in pavement. It hangs in the tower alone with 4 half wheels and sustain'd with a huge frame of timber. It sound but upon High Festivals as for singing an obig't [?] upon the anniversary of some of the Dukes of Normandy. They were forc't to build a tower for it, out of a tax that was laid upon all butter sold in the Lent, and so cal'd the Butter Tower. Opposite to this is another tower which is said to bee built by the English. I read the word God in letters of gold on the one side of it.

The front of this church is verry large, and beautifull. On the right hand is carv'd the feast of Herod and the beheading of St John the Baptist, in the midle was the genealogy of our Saviour, on the left hand was the stoning of St Stephen. After this we saw the large Abby of St Toin, all the upper part of the Quier from top to bottom studded with guilded Flower d' L'ys, a fair cloyster, and great conveniencies for the monkes, some of the towers were unfinisht but the late King Lewis the 13th had given the gratuity of 10000 livers yearly toward the compleating of it. I saw the old pallace in which the parlament sate formerly, but they are now remov'd to a better building, wherein are likewise held the Inferior Courts of Judicature, which makes it much frequented by Advocates Councelors and such like which swarm in France wrather more than in England. In a Court amidst this building was the prison for malefactors, and debtors.

On the Key of this citty we saw severall litle woodden houses, for men to watch for the taking of the Kings Excize upon cider and other commodities, and here by the way I think it not amiss to observe to the Reader some particulars of oppression under which these poore people labor by reason of so great a burden of Excize. In the first place their Grand Signior (as they stile him) takes 15 livres for every tunn of this liquor that is vended, 6 livres annually upon every Hackney horse, 2 pistolls for every beevier, 4 livres for a calfe, 8 for a sheepe, 10 sou's for a lambe. He uses the sole monopoly of salt which he unconscionably sells to the people for 30 livres a bushel when it does not stand him in above one and a half the making. When he comes to any towne by his prerogative he demands candels, vinegar, salt, fuel and such like, besides a present is given him by the Magistrates least hee prove too lavish in these things. Besides hee uses a kind of free quarter for his souldiers all the time of his stay. I could heare of nothing that scap'd the tiranny of Excize but corn. So that the pesants are for the most part brought to deaths doore to support the luxury and ambition of this haughty monarch, and milions of them cut off with as litle concern as a nest of hornets, or pismires.

On the 24th of 7br I left this city and with the messenger took horse for NeuChatto a ville where we lodg'd that night, the cuntry generally plow'd land small loose stones lying upon the ground; a long the highway side great store of aple and pare trees. Comming out of the towne wee beheld the bodies of severall malefactors hanging within a wall for theft. We left this place before day-breake, and a mile without the towne upon the first springing of light upon the brow of a hill we spi'de a miserable poore hermit comming out of his cell and making towards the towne below, his leggs bare, his cowle of sack-cloth sadly patch't. The cuntry for the most part hilly, all the brows of the hills finely fringed with woods. This poor towne was fortified with an old totterd wall. We rode through a wood of beeches which continued shadowing of us for above a mile together. At length we came to dinner to a verry poore towne called Blangee being still in Normandy, and here I thought it verry strange that this meane towne consisting of about 40 thacht houses should bee in-compass'd with a brick wall. We reckon'd 6 leagues betweene Neuchatle and this place. Leaving the towne of Blanche we passt over a deale of corn ground, where we found them sowing contrary to our custome; here the man does not follow the plow, but the land having been plow'd for some time and a plentifull shower following after, the corn is then loosely thrown and scatterd upon the ground and afterward harrowed.

We now enter'd Picardy and lodg'd that night at Abbeville. This is a large towne about the bigness of Reading with us, tis allso noted for cloth-working, and fire-arms. The river running through it is cal'd the Some. About a mile from hence we saw a woman begging in the highway, and wallowing in the dirt. She was so eaten with the pox that scarse the figure of her face remain'd. Early on the 26 Instant we journeyed towards Montrell, leaving the towne of St Valery on the left, being a litle seaport. Afterwards we went by a large mansion belonging to one of the presidents of Paris, and so by the great abby of Faramonte; this was many years since, besieg'd by the Spaniards, who fir'd, and demolisht great part of it, but relief comming from Abevile they were forc'd to quitt it. We came to dinner to Montrel which is well fortified for feare of Spanish incursions, but of it self poore with a litle mean Fauxburgh. The cuntry continued plow'd land, and here and there wooddy till we came to Frankee where we lodg'd for this night. On the 27th Instant we left this miserable raggid village, before day-light and went towards Boloigne. We rode over the sandy hills and so came downe in view of the sea on the left hand, the towne stands upon a hill, and is well immur'd with stone, the houses of the same, but of a low building, a small Fauxburgh stragling downe from the towne to the sea-side, which flows in in a narrow nook betweene the sand-hills.

At the bottom of this stands a fort to command the harbour which is mightily annoyed with sands. The upper part of the towne seem'd verry strong, having an old fort, or chattou likewise to defend it; but the hills towards Calais seeme to command it. Here is continually kept a garrison. This night we reach't Calais and on the morrow morning went off in the paquet-boat for England.

Omnia nil sunt

5

A JOURNEY INTO SCOTLAND

A journey taken from London into Scotland Anno 1674

O N THE 30TH of July this yeare we left this citty about 3 of the clock in the afternoone, and went that night to Hatfield. The next day we journeyed through Hartfordshire, Stephenage and along by Seaven-burie Hills, which are supposed to bee the burying places of Faustinus the Roman and his soldiers slain in fight against Caractacus the Brittain, and so we came to Baldock in the same county. Hence we went through Bugden where stood an antient castle building belonging to the See of Lincoln, the cuntry seeming as if it were subject to bee deepe and morish. We left Whitlesey Mere in view on the right hand; and by the first of August being Saturday night we arrived at the litle city of Peterburrow, a flat cuntry about it and generally floated in the winter. The towne is old, and ill-built, only a commodious Market-House erected in the midle.

Here is a large jurisdiction belonging to the ecclesiasticks, they having the power of thirty two villages round about in cases criminall. The cathedrall here though plain, yet decent, tis most noted for the interment of Katherine Par,[72] and Marie Queen of Scots that strumpet that defil'd this nation with her infamous linage; some other meane remarks as the tomb of the Sexton Scarebabe, and that of the midwive with this comicall epitaph

> Here lies a midwife brought a bed,
> Deliveress delivered –

with an old monument in remembrance of severall monkes massacred by the Danes.

Monday morning we took horse and left this place, and rode by a fair new-built seat belonging to Mr Francis St Johns cal'd Thorp and so to Stanford.

72 John Walker has remembered the wrong Queen Katherine; Katherine of Aragon was buried in Peterborough cathedral.

Comming hither we passt by a large seat belonging to the Earles of Exceter cal'd Burleigh.

Stanford[73]

THIS IS A large towne, and for the mosr part built of stone. It stands in 3 counties at once viz Rutland, Lincoln, and Northamptonshire. It was formerly an university the scholars of Oxford upon the scholars of Oxford (sic) upon some distast taken there removed hither, and to this very day by the statutes of the university are obliged by oath not to practise any of the sciences in this towne. We baited here and immediately from hence took our way through Rutlandshire, a barren, heathy like cuntry, and so by Horn-park belonging to my Lord Cambden and so that night being the 3rd of August to

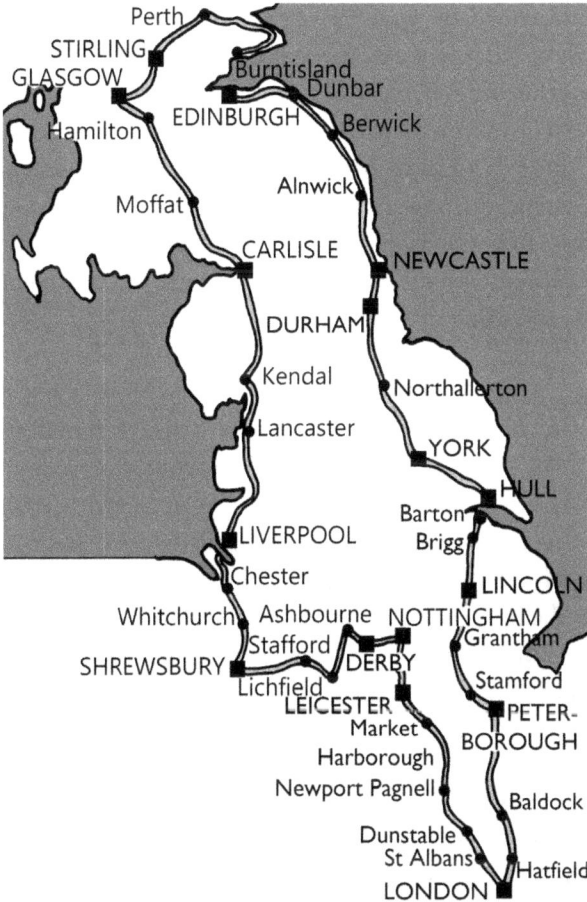

73 Stamford.

Grantham

AN OLD BEGGARLY towne wherein was litle of observation but St Maries church with a verry high beautifull steeple. We departed hence in the morning and travaile'd through a champaign desolate cuntry neither catle, nor tillage to bee seen for many miles, and this evening being the 4th came to the decayed city of Lincoln.

Lincoln

THE PRINCIPALL AND midle part whereof does apertain to the Duchy of Lancaster, the rest but meanely built, and thinly inhabited. The principall sight here was the cathedrall, which presents a verry spatious front, adorn'd with the effigies of some of the Mercian kings sitting under a canopy, or pavilion. We ascended the tower to see the great bell cal'd Tom, which was cast in the 8th of King James as appears by the inscription on it. This towne likewise shows the ruines of a large castle.

On the 5th Instant about 3 of the clock in the afternoon we left this citty passing through a heathy barren cuntry, and lodg'd the night at a poore place cal'd Glandford-Bridge,[74] the next day being the 6th continuing still in Lincolnshire after the same manner we came to Barton Ferry 11 miles distance. We ferried over the Humber which parts the two counties Lincoln and Yorkshire, and came that night to

Hull

HERE WE REMAIN'D all the 7th, and were well accommodated, the towne is not nigh so large as Plymouth; the fortification is but ordinary an old brick-wall erected in the raigne of Henry 8. At Beverly Gate side it seems strongest, having there a double trench two draw-bridges; and a ruinous horn-worke on the left hand; but the chiefest security is that they may drowne it all about. This is the prime port of Yorkshire but much decayed in trade.

On the 8th Instant we left this place, and travail'd through a barren cuntry and came to York that night.

Yorke

HERE WE FOUND a large citty but poore and despicable, having litle trade belonging to it; 'twas our fortune to come here at the Assize time which added some small lustre to the place; the shireve had married one of the Duchess of Yorks gentlewomen and so obtain'd the place by his Highnesses favour.

74 Glanford Bridge or Brigg; Barton-upon-Humber.

At the castle was a fair new-building for the Assize House, a round old building standing upon a hill by it which they call the Tower. After this we went to see the cathedrall which I conceive to bee the largest and fairest in England, divers tombstones with old inscriptions. Here we saw a Chapter House of curious artifice, the top being a large circular arch without any colume to support it, the windows pretty entire and well painted, having been preserv'd by Fairfax at his taking the towne. At the entrance into the Chapter House was this verse in Saxon letters guilded. *Ut Rosa flos florum sic est Domus ista Domorum.* From the middle tower of the cathedrall we took a prospect of the citty. It's inviron'd with a firm stone wall, but for the most part poorly built. My Lord Fretsvill is the Governor. We remain'd till the 11th in the morning, and din'd that day at Topcliff passing over a fair bridge over the river Swale, and lay that night at Northallerton, the next day being the 12th we din'd at Yuckly[75]: the ride betweene York and this place continued verry craggy and ruffe with broken causeys. The cuntry for the most part thinne of people and those verry poore. By the evening we reach't

Durham

THE RODE HITHER continued bad the cuntry desolate scarse a tree to bee seen in many miles riding. About 2 miles distance before we came to this citty we crosst a spatious valley the ground black, and heathy abounding much with cole which gives it the epithite of Black-Durham. It lies upon the river Weere, and is compact and well built, standing betweene a theater of hills. The castle which is the Bishops pallace, and the cathedrall are seated upon a spot of ground like a peninsula, the first is large and loftily built, containing the tombs of Venerable Bede and St Cutbert. By their copes the churchmen here seem'd to bee somwhat spiced with popery. The last bishop Dr Cossins founded here a neate and elegant library for publick use, the pallace had been repair'd at this bishops cost, but at this present alltogether unfurnisht. In the whole is denoted much of antient power and state.

On the 14th Instant we departed from hence, and went through a heathy and open cuntry, abounding with coales all round. We passt by a fair seat cal'd Lumly Castle[76] belonging to the Lord of that name, out of whose park comes the best coales in all these parts. I fogott to observe one thing before that at the upper end of the great-hall belonging to the Bishops pallace, there hung the picture of the Martyr Charles the first with this inscription *Qui tanta mala tulit.* Qui tanta bona fecit which moved us to laughter, to see

75 Oakley Cross on the road at West Auckland.
76 Lumley Castle.

that mercenary prelates will uphold any thing for preferment. This being but a small dayes journey we came early to

New-Castle

THIS TOWNE IS large, full of verry poore people equall to what we see in France, having no dependance but upon the colemines, and keeles which serve to bring the coles up to the ships and the towne. It is inviron'd with an old thick stone wall, but decayed as most of the works of England are, much up hill, and down-hill and in some parts extreme steepe, comming off of one part of the wall to come into the towne we venter'd downe break-neck staiers, a place of great danger. The buildings are good and for the most part stone, like those at Durham, the Change is beautifull, containing a fair hall, and a large Council roome, both pav'd with black and white marble. At the gate over the bridge stands the effigies of this king with this fawning inscription

Restitutio Regis est Solamen Gregis.

Likewise we saw a large old church. The Tyne here is a brave large river, but the mouth of it incommoded with sand, and the hulls of some ships that were sunke thereabouts by stress of weather.

On the 14th Instant in the afternoone we rode away to Morpith,[77] where we lodg'd that night, and in the morning being Sunday view'd a small old ruine'd castle apertaining to the Earle of Carlisle. Sunday after dinner being the 15th Instant, we rode to Anwick, having for the last half-dozen miles the sea in view on the right hand, the cuntry continuing verry barren and heathy only in some places where they had burn'd the turf a good crop of graine. Here we lodged this night. The towne is verry poore, having had none of the Earles of Northumberland to inhabit their antient large castle here for a long time; this denotes much magnificence still, the land for a matter of 20 miles together all belonging to them. From an exploit donne before this castle, which was killing the King of Scots by running a spear in his eye is derived the name of the Percy's.

On the 16th Instant we left this place, and travail'd through a gossy wild cuntry, hilly, and full of stones, having the sea, and Fern Isles[78] in our view. We passt by an old decayed castle standing as it were upon the shore cal'd Dunsleburgh belonging to the Lord Gray. At last we came to bait at an extreme poore village cal'd Belford where we could have neither wine nor beere, the

77 Morpeth; Alnwick.
78 Farne Islands.

people all looking hollow, and meager as if they had not eaten in a month. I remember the woman of the house told us she scarse saw a stranger in a month notwithstanding this is the grand thoroughfare betweene the 2 Kingdomes. After 2 miles riding from hence we came in view of Holy Isle on the right hand, and Chivet Hills on the left and so to Barwick.

Barwick[79]

THIS WAS FORMERLY a Scotch towne, and lies on 'tother side the River Twede so that we passt over a long stone bridge to come to't. It is small and poorly built lying upon a nook open to the sea, great rocky hills about it, the river is not great but affords plenty of salmon fishing, the herring fishing not so plentifull here as it ha's been. We lodg'd at the *Feathers* and in the morning went to see the fortification of the towne, which were verry bad and ruinous towards the sea, but at the higher part of the towne toward Scotland, it being a fortification made by Queene Elizabeth consisting of a firm stone wall and regular bastions, reaching allmost to Tweede; it is somwhat ruinous, having never been repair'd since the dayes of Oliver, for all the King injoyes his owne again; the trenches are choak't up and the earth generally fallen in, the draw bridges all so broken that it is dangerous for horses to pass over, and that which is verry observable that in the time of the Dutch Warr that in the time of the Dutch Warr (sic) they kept but one company here, and now in time of peace they kept five as if twere done designedly to grieve and burden the towne; for at this time they had runne 1200£ into the debt of the poore inhabitants, many of the souldiers having not received any pay in 17 months, insomuch that they took provisions from the market people upon trust. Most of the old brass-guns taken away from the garrisons in the late Dutch Warrs, and no care taken to restore them there remain'd not above 20 guns mounted upon the platforms, and those for the most part small and upon broken carriages, whereby the garrison is become weake and inconsiderable. All the storehouses, viz: brewhouse bakehouse etc built by the Queene for the supply of the garrison, are decay'd, and gonne to ruine. We heard that the townsmen had all their arms taken out of their houses by order of my Lord Witherington the Governor, and were all laid up in Sir Thomas Hazestons house a noted papist.

On the 19 Instant we left this place and rode through Loutham[80] being a barren hilly cuntry lying upon the German ocean. We passt by the towne of Douglass and so through Sketraugh a litle raggid place and so we came that night to –

79 Berwick-upon-Tweed.
80 Lothian. Skateraw.

Dumbarr

THIS IS A litle old stone-built towne with indented gable ends. It subsists most upon herring fishing, lying open to the sea. The peere was made of loose stone somewhat like that at Lime but not neere so large. Upon a rock in the sea stood the ruines of an antient castle, and about a mile into the sea lay the Bass Island which Lauderdale had perswaded the king to purchase of Ramsey the provost of Edenburgh for 10000£. A litle without the towne they show'd us my Lord Roxburroughs garden into which Oliver Cromwell drew his forces the night before he ingage'd the Kirk army who lay to intercept his march for England. In the church they show'd us a lofty tomb erected for the old Earle of Dumbar treasuror to King James. About this place was good plenty of barly, and oates. On the 20th we departed hence and came to Linton and passt over the north-Tyne, and so through Preston towne and by the salt works cal'd Preston-pans and so to Musleburrough[81] wherein stood a large seat belonging to the Earle of Twivedale.[82] The roade now began to open, and grew sandy, and deepe and by 3 in the afternoone we arrived at their metropolis Edenburgh.

Edenburgh

WE ENTRED THE citty, and lodg'd at the *Salutation* just within Kannigate which is port divides the citty from the suburbs, the buildings strong and massie all of stone, the fronts made out with deale board, and round holes cut in them, out of which the people look as if they were standing in the pillory; the staiers of their houses come all out into the streete after an ill-favor'd manner. It is verry populous which is easie to bee seen, the people having litle imployment within dores are for the most part walking. It consists of one large streete reaching above a mile in length viz: from the foot of the hill to the brow therof, on each side of the hill runne downe litle, narrow, nasty lanes which they call closes; from Kannigate to the castle they call the High Streete, about the midle wherof stands a guilded cross, but few of the buildings showing any state, but for the most part like those in the meaner streets at Paris, excepting deale-board fronts. The castle is situated upon a rock and might bee made allmost impregnable with litle art but long time, and neglect has brought it much to ruine and decay, hardly 20 gunns mounted. Here are arms for neere 40000 men, in the castle one extreme large gunne of iron which had crak't the wall in shooting off. The towne is ill accommodated for water having no river at all belonging to it.

81 Musselburgh.
82 Tweedale or Teviotdale?

Afterwards we went to Holy-Roode House, where we saw the great expence Lauderdale had put the Exchequer of Scotland too, having pulled downe the antient pallace of their kings, as not compleat enough for his grandeur, and ha's erected a verry faire building of stone, which ha's put the king to 50000£ expence; there remaines onely of the old building a large chappel, a rude built gate, and some part of the old front with bar'd windows, and the chamber of Queene Anne with A:R: guilded upon the wall. We saw the trone church, and the cathedrall indifferent buildings, in the later not the least of ornament, or ceremony as with us. Here are 14 bishops to this place, but the people in all parts highly dissenting from them abhorring any thing that ha's but the least show of popery. The College here is but ordinary building, like some old Hall in Oxford; but the Library contain'd many good books, and rarities: the learned Buchanans skull. A ms [manuscript] of the Bible in Greeke preserved out of the reliques of that at Alexandria. A horn grown out of the hand of an old woman with a silver plate and an inscription annext to it. The students were no gowns but go loose as they do at Leyden, the women for the most part go in plods. The aire here abouts is certainly verry unwholsome, for about the 20th of August within an hour after sunne sett, the citty was cover'd with as thick fogs, as London is in the midle of December.

On the 24th Instant being a rainy day, we sent our horses for Sterling there to remaine till we came about; we took coach for Lith[83] a little towne upon the sea side lying about a miles distance from Edenburgh, where the merchants use to land their goods. In the way hither I remember we saw the bodies of severall malefactors hanging upon gibbets. From hence we took boat for Burn't Island being about 7 miles over.

Burnt Island

HERE WE WERE well lodg'd, and accommodated and solac't our selves with the musick of the place, an extraordinary bagpipe and on the 25th Instant wrode along the seaside in the cuntry of Fife having prodigious rocks on the left hand, off of which one of their kings, Alexander the 3rd broke his neck a hunting. Passing by we saw a litle spring issuing out of the rocks upon the hollow of a mussle shell; the waters are medicinall, and much frequented by the ladies of Edenburgh, and the cuntry thereabouts and is cal'd their spaw. We came to Kirkande[84] and to Dysart seeming a verry old towne and so to Wemes, where we baited upon herrings. From thence to Lesly where we saw a new built seat on the side of a hill belonging to the Lord Wrothy's the Chancelor,

83 Leith.
84 Kirkcaldy; Wemyss; Leslie.

whome we had seen before passing over in his yeacht to Lith. I remember on a tombstone in the churchyard of this parrish we saw many freakish inscriptions; amongst the rest was a tombstone baring this: on the one side of the stone sett at the head of the grave was 'Here lies an Honest Man' on the other side was 'Here lies an Honest Woman his Wife'. It is observable here that the women in this cuntry never change their names upon marriage. Hence we proceeded where we saw a pretty litle pallace built by James the 6th where he us'd to lodge when he came upon his passtimes of hawking and hunting. The Earle of Athos is the present House-keeper. Tis much gonne to ruine at this time.
From this place (sic)

St Johnstowne

THIS LIES AT the foot of the Highlands and was antiently cal'd Perth, the mountains reach up within the cloudes all above the towne. From the tops of these we saw the great bon'd Highlanders come downe and barter for tobacco, with ducks, and poultry and such small traffiq. It consists of 2 large streets; and ruinous building with old boarded fronts, a decayed kirke, with seats for the severall artificers of the towne, their professions wrote upon each seat; 'tis allso observable here that most great churches contain a seat for the King peculiarly. Tis seated upon a faire river cal'd Tey. Here we beheld the rubbish of an old cittadel erected by Oliver to check this part of the cuntry; this we reckon'd the heigth of our journy, having come upon the north-east side of England hither, we determin'd to retourn by the northwest; so on the 26th Instant we departed hence, and took a Guide with us through a wretched cuntry of rocks, and hills, and barrenness to Stirling, having only met with some poore village about the half-way cal'd OchterArde[85] wherein was a poore church in which they told us the great Montrose was inter'd, and bad accomodation at the house of one David Steward, no doubt a branch of some of the Royall Family, they being very numerous in these parts and as poore and as shabby as the meanest sort of people. In this place is an old house belonging to the Crowne in the keeping of the Earle of Athos.

Sterling

IN THE EVENING we came over Sterling-Brigge where so many batles have been fought, and came into the towne and lodg'd in an old stone building up in a tower at one John of Kilboyes a high sounding name. This is by some cal'd Striveling, or Sterling, our accompt of money being taken from hence, being first coin'd in the castle of this towne, this at that time being the utmost

85 Auchterarde.

terminus of the English Conquest. The River Forth runs by it, it is seated upon a hill, old stone building cover'd with slat, one fair street leading up to the Earle of Marrs house. Going up to the castle we saw a fair house erecting for the Earle of Argyle, who upon the intercession of his friend Lauderdale, was restor'd to all properties by his Majesties favour. We enter'd and saw the castle which is a goodly building standing upon a high rock, a litle parke at the foot of it with a small parcel of bald trees. It was for the most part erected by James the 5th. In it a large chapel built for the christning of prince Henry, and a spatious rome for the entertaining the English nobles sent by Queen Elizabeth as her representatives at the solemnity. They show'd us the ship that came in upon wheeles, and discharg'd her gunns as they sate at dinner, it seem'd to me like an old Tub. Here I saw they would not trust the Militia with their arms, they deliver 'um out only just for the day of Muster and as soone as ever they have donne take 'um in again. This being the 27th Instant we left the towne and travail'd over a rocky boggy More so that it prov'd a tedious dayes journey to –

Glascow[86]

T HIS IS A university, and is rekon'd the flower and beauty of all Scotland, the streets large, and straite; the publick buildings very ornamentall. Here is the best cathedrall in all Scotland, a neate well-built College, a large Tolbuth with these verses engraven on it

Hac Domibus odit, amat, punit, conservat, honorat
Justitiam, pacem, crimina, jura, probos.

Tis seated upon the River Kloide, a faire stone bridge over it. Here they were preparing a stock for a fishing trade, and Lauderdale seiz'd all by virtue of the Kings prerogative. Twas a pretty peece of news they told us here, that Argyle had leave from the king to levy any number of men not exceeding 10000 to recover the possession of the Island of Mol from young Macklen whose father had mortgaged it to the old Earle of Argyle. Hee accordingly levied a considerable number but the young man never stood it out but surrendred upon terms.

On the 28th we proceded on our journey, the way continuing verry bad and passt by an old castle belonging to the Marquess of Douglass, continuing still in Kloidisdale, and came to –

86 Glasgow on the River Clyde.

Hamilton

HERE WE BAITED being a neate litle towne and had good accommodation. We took an outside view of Duke Hamiltons pallace which was a lofty building well battlemented affording much of state, and pleasure: behind the house stood a grove of pines, fruit-gardens about which was the only brick-wall I saw in Scotland, groves and grotto's for diversion, warren, and parke, so that in the whole they reckon'd about sixteene mile incompasst with a firm wall.

We went from hence, and that night to a wretched village cal'd Lismihagi;[87] here we had sad lodging, and scarse any provision, nothing but Aqua vitae and water for drinke, and no provender for our horses, the verry rats were like to eat up my Companions coat for hunger. The 29th we went onwards, passing through a sad boggy stony cuntry still in Kloidisdale and so to Douglass, then to Craford, and with a Guide went over the mountains that night to

Mophet[88]

A LAMENTABLE POORE village houses all coverd with turf instead of thatch; it is noted for a medicinall well a mile distant, the whole towne would afford no provender for our horses, we were constrain'd to buy a litle course mast, and boile it. We were a litle diverted by a prating land-lady, who gave us an accompt of the apprehending the phanaticks upon the Mosse at their meeting by Linlithgow.

We left this place on the 30th being Sunday and pass'd over the rapid River Anan, and so enter'd Anandale and came to Eglesagi[89] a miserable place where we found some small refreshment, and through a boggy morish wild cuntry (by the help of a Guide, who had been a theife upon the Border) wee gott that night to Greatny[90] in Anandale. Here we lodg'd in a low roome upon straw-beds, no window for any light but what appear'd at the crannies of the doore which we made fast with a litle stick as they do the gates of a field. We were now come upon the West Borders; early in the morning we got up, and took our landlord for our Guide. We touch'd upon Lidisdale, and so we were conducted over the rivers of Eske and Eden (all along being a verry distressed cuntry) and by dinner came to the citty of

87 Lesmahagow.
88 Moffat.
89 Eaglesfield?
90 Gretna.

Carlisle

BY THE WAY hither we were show'd the Burgh or hill on which Edward 1 died retourning from his conquests in Scotland. We arrived here the last day of the Assizes; tis but a litle towne but totally inviron'd with a wall, a small cathedrall in it of red stone, in part demolisht. Afterwards we went to see the castle which is but a small thing built for the most part by Queene Elizabeth the chief gunns on the Battery hers too. This towne formerly much infested by the Scots so that it remains a custome to this day to present all the judges attendance with daggers, and the shireeve ha's it allow'd upon accompt. This is the metropolis of Cumberland. Here we remained all the 31 Instant, and the next day being the 1 of 7br [September] wee baited at Perith[91] a pretty good towne in which stood a demolisht castle belonging to the Crowne. In the church-yard of this place they show'd us (a thing of wonder, as they call it) which was the tomb of Giant sett with a pyramid at each end, and severall great stones betweene 'um. The cuntry was for the most rocky, so that the wayes are difficult to pass. We went over the River Eden, and enter'd Westmorland, and that night took up our lodging at a place cal'd Shap. The next day being the 2nd Instant wee baited at Kendale or Kintdale lying upon the River Kint and the most trading towne in all the county of Westmorland which is but a small thing being as it were one continued rock. From hence by night we came to –

Lancaster

'TIS BUT A small towne and much decayed, it lies upon the River Lune from whence it is denominated. My Lord of Darby a haughty, ambitious man finding the towne would not comply with him in the advancing of Tiranny in the old kings cause in the late warrs came with a body of horse and burn't it downe in revenge. Here is scarse any thing observable, and old ruinous castle belonging to John of Ghaunt [who held the principallity) with a rotten chair which they call his seate. We had excellent accomodation here and reasonable, the way here is ordinaries. The towne being throngd with the comming of the shireeve to the Assizes we went from hence on the 3rd Instant and lodg'd that night at Gasthen,[92] where we view'd a litle castle belonging to the Earles of Darby ruine'd in the late warrs, but of a very regular fortification. Hence on the 4th Instant wee baited at Preston, a good towne lying upon the River Ribble

91 Penrith.
92 Garstang?

and that night to Wiggon,[93] a towne of excelent accommodation; the cuntry continuing plentifull but a deepe soile.

On the 5th leaving this place we went over the River Douglass, where they told us of the ingagement betweene the Earle of Darby and Colonel Lilburn in the late times. We proceeded and din'd at Prescot, and lay that night at –

Lever-poole

A SMALL TOWNE but it much incroaches upon the city of Chester for trade, insomuch that the kings customs here are double to what they are there. It lies upon an arm of the sea, which divides that and Cheshire. It increases in building which is of a good model, and all of brick. They were erecting a small exchange here. Wee took a view of the decayed castle belonging to my Lord Mollineux, and an old stone tower by the sea-side which is my Lord of Darby's. Wee rested here all the 6th Instant being Sunday, having found Lancashire throughout a plentifull good cuntry, and the best I have mett withall in England. On the 27th wee ferried over to the rock in Cheshire, and wrode that night to the citty –

Chester

THIS IS A pretty large towne, and was antiently a place of great traffique and esteeme, but tis much decayed by reason of a hazardous bar'd channel. Here and there tis well built, but for the most part antient paper edifices, with ill-favor'd peazo's or passages along the side. Tis surrounded with an old battlemented wall, which is kept well in repaire by oficers cal'd Muringers; it lies upn the River Dee. We saw the cathedrall which is but a meane structure, of red-stone and greatly out of repaire, likewise a poore castle commanded by Sir Jeoffery Shakerly. At the entrance over the gare they show'd us a mans hand nail'd up who threw at a judge upon passing sentence against him. The commicall effigies of Hugh Lupus an antient Earle of this place, which is sett out upon High dayes at the entrance to the church; an old Roman altar that had been dugg out of some ruines. Here are eight parish churches.

From hence on the 8th Instant wee proceeded to Whitchurch (a ruff way) where we took up our lodging that night, this was the first towne in Shropshire we came too, it is now the Earle of Bridgwaters, but was formerly belonging to the Talbots Earles of Shrewsbury who were founders of the church, as may bee seen by the carving over the portall. On the 9th Instant wee departed and went that night for Shrewsbury –

93 Wigan.

Shrewsbury

LYING IN A faire valley along upon the River Severn, girt about the midle with an antient wall with watch-towers but decayed and unfitt for a siege; a sad ruin'd castle which the king had bestowed upon the Lord Newport. We went to the old Abby-Church where we saw an old figure or monument belonging to Richard Montgomery once Earle of this place, which had been losst, had not the care of the Heraulds in theire visitation in the raigne of Charles the first restor'd it again. Like Chester it consists much of poore paper building. It was formerly the chiefe seate of the Lluellins princes of Wales.

On the 10th Instant wee went away to Newport in the same county it being still well woodded, and not withstanding a bad way we came that night to –

Stafford

A VERRY ANTIENT towne scituate upon the River Trent, in which was nothing but a large church, and Towne-House erected by Queene Elizabeth. On the morrow being the 11th Instant we went hence and set forward for the citty of –

Lichfield

HERE WE BEHELD a fair cathedrall restored and beautified by the care of Bishop Hacket, wherein he had a neate monument. Here was the shrine of St Shad, and a lofty guilded spyre. No river about it, 'tis much bigger than Stafford, and a good gracefull citty for building. The soile of this cuntry is for the greatest part cold and clawy. We travel'd through a great part of it, and on the 12th Instant went away and baited at Uxcester[94] and so to Ashburn[95] that night just within the borders of Darbyshire. Here we lodg'd intending to have gonne to the Peake but finding it too farr without the conveniency of fresh horses which we could not obtain, wee alter'd our resolutions and on the next day being the 13th gott to –

Darby

WHICH STANDS UPON the wide River of Derwent. Speede has's made a wonder of a chappel built upon a bridge over the river, but we found it only upon arches at the side of the bridge and but a meane building. Wee saw Allhallows church with a high well built tower, first beganne at the charge of

94 Uttoxeter.
95 Ashbourne.

the young men and maides of the towne as appears by an inscription on the outside of it. In this church stood a marble monument erected for the old Earle of Devonshire and his Countess their figurees standing upright under an arch of black marble but rudely carv'd and too much of the Tuscan order. Here was a well built shire Town-House all the rest but ordinary so on the 14th Instant wee went our way for –

Nottingham

A VERRY GOOD and ample towne, for the most part of new-built brick building; the ruines of the antient castle here were observable in which was Mortimers Hole, so much spoken off by our Chronologers, and many other strange meander hew'd out of the rocks, and so allso in the park which lay at the foot of the hills. It seems the Duke of New-Castle had purchas'd it of the Duke of Buckingham, and is now pulling downe the ruines and levying the hill intending to erect a stately fabrick instead thereof. It lies on the River Trent. We were diverted here with one pretty artifice which was spinning of glass, making of it fusil, and moulding of it into all shapes with variety of colours. In the chief church we saw a well contriv'd monument erected for the Earle of Clare. The cuntry round about fruitfull and pretty well woodded. From hence on the 15th wee proceeded to –

Leicester

A POORE TOWNE depending upon nothing but the rode and a litle manufacture of worsted stockins. Wee went to St Margarets the Mother Church, but nothing in it remarkable. The cuntry wild and claiy abounding much with beanes. Few seates of note.

On the 16 wee baited at Harburrow[96] lying upon the borders of this shire, the counties all this way abounding with coales and alabaster. From hence to Northampton, a towne affording nothing but the ruines of a castle, and demolisht walls, presently after the blessed Restauration.

On the 17th wee lodg'd at Newport-panel[97] and on the 18th wee baited at Dunstable in Bedfordshire. Comming hither wee pass'd by a faire seate on the left hand belonging to the Earles of Bedford, and another on the right belonging to Sir John Duncombe. To St Albons that night, and the next day for London being the 19th.

Nos hæc novimus esse nihil

96 Harborough.
97 Newport Pagnel.

6
A GRAND TOUR OF FRANCE

A seconde voyage beganne in March into France in order to the making the Grand Tour being in Anno 1675

MARCH THE 25TH wee sett out and arrived at Calais on the 27th, and on the 29th took the Messenger, and in 5 dayes came to Paris having had ill weather most part of the way. Wee mett with litle observable as wee passt. Bulloigne[98] is but an old meane fortification. Monterell much stronger having a morass all on one side of it. Abbeville a verry large towne but inconsiderable for strength; here wee saw a regiment of foot march through to goe for Champaigne. At Poy an old castle belonging to the Duke of Crequy. Bovoy a great towne and an episcopall see pretty well seated the hills all round cover'd with vinyards.

The first weeke wee came to Paris, being Easter, and fowle weather wee saw but litle except (at the Grand Augustines upon the Qoy)[99] the scene of our Saviours praying in the Garden and his Disciples sleeping carelessly about Him, and God the Father appearing above in Glory, and such kind of superstitious passtime.

Afterwards wee saw the College of the Sorbone Doctors and their chappell which was founded by Cardinal Richlieu, and then the College of the Quatre Nation instituted by Cadinall Mazarine, but left as yet unfinisht, here was the Cardinalls Library rang'd in a faire gallery; so to the church of the Abby of St Germains, where wee beheld the chappell that is sett apart for the monuments of the Scotch Douglasses that have served in the French warrs; and the tombe of Cassimire King of Poland (that enter'd into religion here) sitting under a pavilion of state and offfering up his crowne and scepter to Heaven.

98 Boulogne; Montreuil; Poix-de-Picardie; Beauvais.
99 Quai?

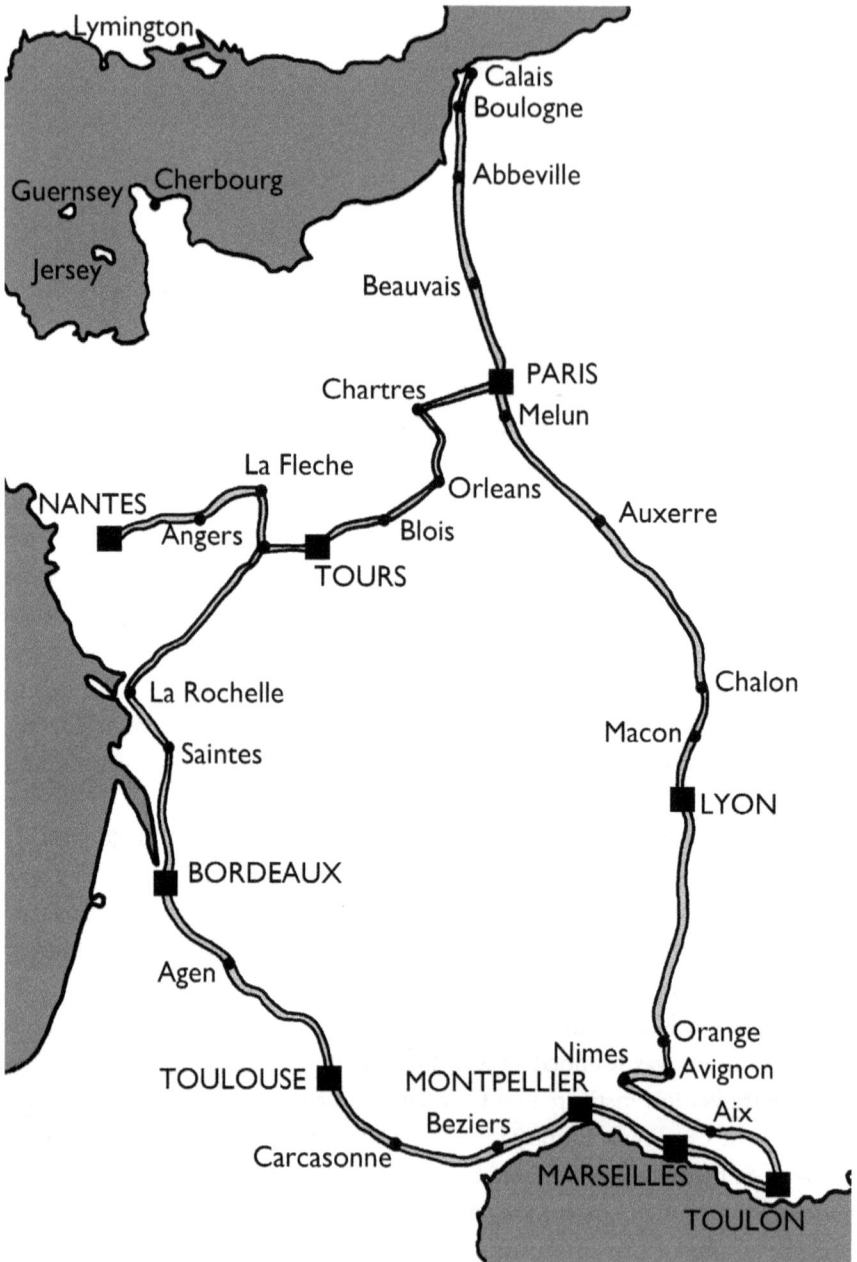

Lymington
Calais
Boulogne
Abbeville
Guernsey Cherbourg
Beauvais
Jersey
Chartres PARIS
Melun
La Fleche
Orleans
NANTES Auxerre
Angers Blois
TOURS
Chalon
La Rochelle Macon
Saintes LYON
BORDEAUX
Agen
Orange
Nimes Avignon
TOULOUSE MONTPELLIER Aix
Beziers
Carcasonne MARSEILLES
TOULON

Gardemuable

WEE SAW THIS here, which containes great riches, and variety of large
roomes laden with massey plate, many figures of silver, as Daphne
and Apollo, the ravishing of the Sabinian Women, David with his sling, other
placecss heapt with imbroiderd beds, and hangings, and pictures in various

Anjou	[Angers]
Artois	[Arras]
Brittany	[Rennes]
Burgundy	[Dijon]
Champagne	[Troyes]
Dauphiné	[Grenoble]
Flanders	[Douai]
Guyenne & Gascony (Guiene)	[Bordeaux]
Ile-de-France	[Paris]
Languedoc	[Toulouse]
Normandy	[Rouen]
Picardy	[Amiens]
Poitou	[Poitiers]
Provence	[Aix-en-Provence]
Saintonge	[Saintes]
Touraine (Turene)	[Tours]

French Provinces and their Capitals before 1789

shaded silks. Severall chargers of pure gold, one of 1400l ounces. Basquets of philigrin gold. Servises of plates of christall of the rock others of purpl'd christall rimm'd with gold. Porphiry urns, cups, and bowles of agat jasper and sardonyx. A large basin containing a gallon all of one orient onyx. Our Saviour carv'd in onyx tied with his hands behind him to bee scurged to a christall columne. Abundance of rich armour and arms both guilt stain'd, ingrav'd, and imbosst with may curiosities, amongst which was a large phang of a bore with great gothick letters verry illegible.

Addit to St Dennys

Passing through this towne I took a review of the Treasury, for remembring some of the more noble reliques viz a large boule of agat us'd by Ptolomeus Philadelphus at his Bauhahole and was 30 years ingraving. One of the dishes that K Solomon us'd at his sacrifices in the Temple, sett with rubies and saphirs, and a yore [gore?] all of cristall of the rock which was us'd at his owne table. The face of Julius Cesar (while a child) cutt in agott, and Nero's likewise in white agate.

Sharington[100]

THE NEXT DAY being Sunday, wee went to the church of Sharrington where wee beheld a vast Convention of Hugonotes, which shows what they would come to had they but a toleration; for the residue of this weeke wee were diverted with Scarramuccio and his Italian farse; then the opera at the Palais-Royall in which were represented the inchantments of Medea, the scenes habit, and singing extraordinary.

Next wee saw the king take a review of his Cavalry (before they enter'd the Campaigne) being about 4000 Horse in number spread upon the plaine of St Germains, the K[ing] himself riding betweene every Battalion. They consisted of the Jeau d'Armes, the Guard d Corps, and the Musquetere d'Roy which in all made a faire Equipage. After this wee went to Rouel[101] a seat belonging to the Duchess d'Agilliere in which were fine Grotts and Jett'os, with the prospect of the Mount d'St Valery neatly painted; the skie was here so well expresst, that the birds have been often seen to fly against the wall taking of it for light. Hence we took a view of the Monsieurs pallace at St Clou which was then allmost pul'd downe but a fair new-building erecting in its steede, the gardens large tending downe to the River Seyne, many figures, and cascades. On the right-hand lay a great hill like a chaos.

Bois d'Vincent[102]

THE NEXT DAY wee took coach to see this place, which is large space of ground thick sett with trees whither the parisian gallants resort to take the aire in the evenings as ours doe in Hide-parke, only here was a large Chatteau (and a chapel); here the Dutch prisoners were kept and such sort of beasts as in our Tower. Retourning home wee saw the garden of Monsieur Ramboict, which had verry delightfull walkes, and mazes. The next day wee saw the Comedie of Circe, acted by Monsieurs troope of commedians, which (I thinke) farr exceeded the Opera, especially in the scenes of Venus Temple, and the pallace of the sunne.

We left Paris on the 22nd Instant Old Stile, and took coach for Orleans, which stood us in four crowns a piece wee nourishing our selves; by the way wee passt by a faire seat belonging to Monsieur Colebert, where was held a Fair for all sorts of catle, the place inclosed with a wall; wee dined at Chastres,[103] and that night wee lodg'd at Estampe where were quarter'd many souldiers

---

100   Saint-Germain de Charonne?
101   Rueil now Rueil-Malmaison; Saint-Cloud.
102   Bois de Vincennes.
103   Chastres? Etampes; Toury.

going to the Campaigne. Wee mett great store of bread waggons going thither likewise. The next day wee din'd at Touree, and so to Orleans, a large causey continuing all the way from Paris to this old citty.

Orleans

HERE WEE LODG'D at the Signe of the *Roy d'Suede*, tis an old, large meane built towne having but litle trade, an antique ruinous fortification with a deepe fosse round about it; tis scituate upon the River Loyer[104] over which goes an old fashione'd bridge, about the midle whereof stands (in brass) the figure of the Virgin Mary holding her sonne in her lap after his Crucifixion; on her right hand is Charles the 7th of France kneeling, and the Pusil de Orleans[105] in the same posture girt about the loins with a broad-sword all crown'd with chaplets which is duly performed at her Anniversary or Festivall, which wee had the good-fortune to see while wee remained here; the procession or ceremony being as neeere as I remember in this manner; the severall orders of the Religious proceede according to their places baring their foppish reliques with them in state. The Chanons of the cathedrall likewise in surplices waring garlands upon their wrists. The Intendant of the citty in a scarlet gowne, with the Advocates, and Bourgois in their robes. The old habiliments of the pusil are worne by a lad of about 16 years of age who takes an oath that hee has not losst his pusillage, hee carries a banner in his hand attended with 2 others who doe the like, with variety of musick, and in this manner goe to the bridge where they pay their devotions to the statue of the Holy Virgin and offer up their chaplets of flowers after which the gunns are fir'd for joy; then they retourn into the towne and put him into the Anian or prison[106] for some small time, then they bring him out and feast him at the Mason d'Ville, the next day hee assists (in the cathedrall) at the celebration of Mass at the High Altar with his drawn sword. His reward for all this mumming is only a paire of stockins, and shooes, a hat, and a shirt and 4 livers in money so the sport endeth.

Next wee went to the church of St Croix the cathedrall as I take it, this with many other Religious Houses here have suffer'd much by the hands of the Hugonotes, then to the chappel of the Annunciation which seemes verry regular with a nunnery, adjoining to it, so to the Capuchines Garden and the Chartereux which affords nothing extraordinary. After this wee took coch (sic) and went to La-Fierte[107] a large house belonging to the Marshall

---

104   River Loire.

105   Pucelle d'Orleans celebrates Joan of Ark liberating Orleans in 1429.

106   A church is dedicated to Saint Anian or Aignan in Orleans.

107   La Ferté-St.Cyr.

of that name, being 4 leagues from Orleans, the gardens here were extreme delightfull, and spatious, many canals of water in the middle a basin wider than that at the Thuleries; an orangery verry great, and a brick-wall for fruite neere 800 yards in length. The house of no curious model, but the inside well adorn'd with pictures. As of Joane Queene of Naples, Joane of Arc, old Lot in a purple gowne going in too have carnall knowledge with his daughter, who was spread upon a pallet, the rising of her belly exactly expresst, the other daughter lying at the other end of the rome, and lamps burning, showing a pleasing night piece. In another roome was a nymph sleeping upon her back, covering her privities with her hand. In our retourn wee view'd la-Sourse which is a deepe sub-terraneous issuing of water which feedes the River Loirete. Wee passt through Olivet, and the same night home.

On the 2nd of May Old Stile being Sunday wee took coach for Chatteau-Neuf[108] which lies within the Forrest of Orleans a seate of a pleasant situation, the gardens reaching downe to the side of the river Loyar with jett'os, canals, walkes, wildernesses, and such delights. The house stands upon a moderate ascent at the upper end of the garden, a forse [?fosse] about it the roomes lofty, and large, a gallery with variety of maps, and pictures. It belongs to the Marquess of that name being sonne to one of the four Secretaries of State. In our retourne we saw Chenaillie a house belonging to a protestant gentleman of that name, who had formerly sided with the prince of Conde by which hee was somwhat under hatches, this was but a small house, but the seate, and gardens well contriv'd for melancholly, and contemplation. Wee passed through Jargou and retourned again to Orleans that night. Here wee went to the Tragedy of Sertorius acted with a farse at the end of it cal'd the *Cocu Imaginer*, a meane stage and indifferently acted.

The next day wee went up the steeple of St Croix to view the cuntry which show'd verry pleasant round about; the chief diversions here is walking upon an open Mal lying by the old towne-wall. On the 5th of May early in the morning wee took water, where a litle boy came begging somthing for the sake of St Nicholas, who it seemes is the watermans patron, or Saint. 17 leagues distant from hence is Blois. Wee pass't by Beaujanci[109] where they fabulously relate that the Devil built 'um a bridge, upon condition that hee might have the first creature that passt over, and the inhabitants to delude him tourn'd over a cat; 2 fair seats on each hand of the river belonging to the Intendant of Orleans. By the 7th hour in the evening we arrived ar Blois and lodg'd at the *Cheval Blanc*; continuing still in the province of La Beauce.

108   Chateauneuf-sur-Loire; Jargeau.
109   Beaugency.

Blois

THIS TOWNE IS well seated upon rising ground on the side of the River Loyar, here wee saw a large chatteau, the greatest part whereof was erected by the old Duke of Orleans, who intended it a sumptuous building, but dyed before it was finisht so that now it remains as a great ruine standing upon a hill above the towne. It is at this time belonging to the king. Here was acted that dismall tragedy by Henry 2, on the Duke d'Guise, and the Cardinal his brother; they show'd us the dungeon where the Cardinal was imprison'd and afterward put to death there, with the iron doore therunto, and the chamber where the said duke was expos'd dead to the kings view; then the long gallery built by this Duke of Orleans, and the walk underneath and the 2 gardens lying on each hand thereof in the uppermost 2 fine wells. Beyond the castle the water side the Duke of Orleans caused to bee cast up a bourgh, or hill for a prospect to Chambour[110] which house wee rode to see on the Saturday following. This was built by Francis the first, but not much frequented since the raigne of Henry 4 so that it remaines ruinous and neglected; upon the first approach it presents a stately old Frontispiece of carv'd worke with many lofty turrets adorn'd with crown'd dragons. In the midle stands a large staier-case with a double ascent winding about a wreath'd columne going up many foot above the rest of the building and ending in a cupola; from which you have a pleasant prospect over all the woods of the Forrest which extends it self for some leagues about for the benefit of the kings hunting.

Leaving this wee went for Chevarne[111] where stood a faire seate belonging to the Marquess d'Mouglass Count of this name, who was newly dead so that wee could only see the gardens and not the inside of the house, from the descent of this garden wee saw into five long walkes at once, all cover'd with greene appearing like so many long galleries; from hence wee rode to Beau-Regard, a pretty seate wellwooded with a pleasant flower-garden belonging to one Monsieur Harbie a president of the parlament of Paris, the cuntry round about exteame pleasant. On the 12th Instant leaving Blois wee took boate early in the morning and by noone arriv'd at Amboys being about tenne leagues distance.

Amboys[112]

THIS IS A small village but verry antient, the principall thing in it is the chatteau which formerly did belong to the Cardinal of Amboys, and

110   Chambord.
111   Cour-Cheverny.
112   Amboise; Chenonceaux.

from him it devolve'd to Francis the first. Here in an old chappel hangs up that great raritie of nature, the horns of that vast stagg which was taken in the Forrest of Ardhen in the raigne of Francis the first; they are in heigth twelve foot, in breadth tenn; below these in an iron chaine hangs the neck bone of this monstrous creature. In another chappel at the entrance hang up four of his ribs. Here are severall shrines at which former kings paid their devotions. In a round tower toward the water-side was an old vaulted worke with an arch of bricke, upon which Francis the first did use to ascend in his coach to come up privately into the inner parts of the castle. Here is likewise a well of great depth lin'd with stone, which is so contriv'd that all the offices lie in arches round about it and have windows and holes below one another to let downe bucquets for a supply of water. Without the towne by the river side is a litle promanade sett with trees, for walking in the coole of the evening. In this place wee were mightily deceiv'd by the noise, or croaking of frogs which was extreamly like the crie of a pack of deepe mouth'd hounds. This is the first towne wee came to in the province of Turene. Wee lodg'd at the *Esen* at the bridge foot where wee were well accommodated. Here wee went downe the ladders to see the floating mills upon the river.

On the 14th Instant wee hir'd horses and wrod to Chenausho a house belonging to the Duke d'Vaudosme, being about 2 leagues distant from this towne and lying upon the river Chain.[113] The house is a strong castle building upon arches (cross this river) in which are the kitchin and other convenient offices. In one of the roomes below staiers, wee beheld the picture of Henry 3 drawne at length with this motto underneath *Sævi Monumenta doloris*. But little furniture above stairs, only some shutes of old hangings, in which were the fights of Turnus and Æneas for Lavinia. A gallery in which stood the heads of the Cæsars of large proportion carv'd in marble. In the whole it seemed to bee a verry solitary seate. Departing from hence upon our poore palfryes enduring the heate of the day, by the evening wee arriv'd at Tours 7 leagues distant.

Tours

THIS IS AN old large citty, with ruin'd fortification but the metropolis of Turene. It may be stiled the silken citty, the women wearing more of it here than in any part of France. Wee saw the Moulins d'Soir, which serve for winding it up upon many spindles, which are drawne by a woman who winds at the same time; 4 or 5 others in another roome; which are forc't by a man in a wheele on the outside. Then the weaving mills for making of flower'd silkes.

113   River Cher?

The colenders which are mills of vast weight of iron barrs and timber (drawne by horses) which gives the impression or waving to tabbies, and mohairs rowling underneath upon cylinders. Afterwards to the cathedrall church; at the altar at the upper end of the quire stands a batlement of polisht brass, angels and cherubs of the same fixt on the top. 2 verry beautifull towers of an equal height, in one whereof hang 2 bells of extreme magnitude greater than any that I have seene but that at Rhone. The Mal here is a delightfull being, shady, and coole, and guarded on both sides with a wall, and high banke.

Afterwards wee went to see the old Abby of Marmotie, where they show'd us their reliques viz: a bone of St Markes arme sett in silver with a glass over it; the Sainte Ampulle, or bottle of Holy oyle which does miracles.

On the 21 of this Instant wee left Tours and took boate for Saumur where wee ariv'd that night being 17 leagues distant.

Saumur

THIS IS BUT an ordinary meane-built towne, frequented much by strangers, because of the profession of the protestant religion, which is much in use here, and the Academy. It is cal'd Saumurium upon their submitting to the salt tax upon the condition of having their walls built againe which are now old and ruinous. The streets ly verry crooked, and ill-favour'd to the view.

We saw the antient chatteau standing upon the hill, which gives a prospect over the towne into a pleasant plaine of vinyards; but it lies ruinous and of no validity. The house of the Pere d'Oratoir which is a good plain building, and a convenient garden but the chappell stood unfinisht as to the covering. The garden of the Recolets lies well for melancholy and sedendariness, and affords a prospect to the poet Theophiles Cave.

Fonteveraud[114]

ON THE 27TH Instant wee hir'd horses, and rode to this village, where stands a vast old nunnery that had been founded by some of our English princes. Here in the nunns quire through the grate wee were show'd the tombe of Richard the first cal'd Cour-d'Lyon, and of H.2nd his father, with the effigies of the Countess of Thoulouse kneeling upon the same tombe supported by 2 Lyons, here wee din'd and that night on for –

Richlieu

A NEATE COMPACT litle towne built verry regular, surrounded with a wall and a graft, the vinyards about it are incompass't with a stone walk so

114   Fontevraud.

that it is rocky towards Saumur; yet the towne lies low & unhealthy. After passing through the first streete which is of a good length, you come into a large open space of ground for a market-place on the right-side whereof stands a beautifull church built by the Cardinal. Wee lodg'd at the *Peau d'Or* and the next morning, went to view the magnificant pallace of Cardinal Richelieu, and now belonging to a Duke of that name. The woods belonging to this seate doe as it were imbrace the towne. The pallace seems allmost a square building of the Dorick order; the entrance is a low structure with a terras on the top (giving a prospect to all the rest of the court) and about the midle a large pavilion under which stands the figure of his Master Lewis 13th on the outside, being of white marble, and 3 young Hercules on the inner-side towards the court, with two rostrall columns loaden with navall trophees indicating his being Admirall of France. The inside of the court adorn'd with antique Roman figures sett in neeches of the wall. viz: Scylla, Marius, Julius Cæsar, Agripina, 2 rare imbellisht Venus's, one by Phidias 'tother by the hand of Praxiteles the Grecians 2 slaves of vast proportions (carv'd by Michael Angelo) supporting the frontispiece of the house. A gallery most richly guilded, and painted, all the flower inlaide in which are pourtraide all the actions of this Cardinall under Lewis the 13th being sett in parallel with the Greeke, and the Roman history. The heads of severall emperours, and princes viz: Epaminondus Pyrhus Alexander, Macrime, Papienus with many others all obducted with mantles of Indian jasper, and agate. At the entrance are the pictures of the king, and the cardinall in full proportion on horseback; the head of Julius Cæsar standing on the mantle-tree of the chimney of porphiry cover'd with a mantle of white marble, together with 2 delicate antique Roman urnes of porphiry in wreath'd worke. A table of most costly worke in the midle whereof is sett an agate of 16 inches in length and 9 in breadth, adorn'd with lapis-lazuli, and variety of agates and other stones. At the upper end is the dome pav'd with black, and white marble, with a cupola curiously painted. Here stand the statues of Germanicus, Livia, and old Tiberius appearing verry exquisite to the beholder. The lodgings well painted, and guilded, as the chambers of Lucretia, and Portia so cal'd cause they are pourtraide there the one stabbing herself with a dagger, and the other swallowing of live-coales. Then the cabinet in which are represented the four seasons of the yeare being the emblems of the nobility and court of France. Another chamber wherein stands a porphiry table, and a great porphiry urne of an ovall figure in imbosst high-worke with the heads of Democritus, and Heraclitus of touchstone. A stately chappel wherein was the picture of St Hieronse in mosaick worke.

The upper part of the garden sett with figures and termes in green-neeches with a grott, and a cave close by; long canals, and water-workes, with a spatious Mal. The stables, and out offices are verry noble: behind one of these ranges of building was a pleasant orangery, and litle devises by water a Capuchine ringing a bell, and falling doune to his devotions. Many delightfull views of great length through the woods; wee departed hence the next morning and wrode to Champignee[115] where wee saw a faire church of the Chanonois with painted windows, and reliques, such as 2 or 3 short haires of the Virgin, some drops of Christs blood; and hard by it the remnant of an old chatteau which did belong to the Duchess of Monpensier, and demolisht by the Cardinall for the building of Richelieu hitherto in the province of Poitou.

Hence wee took horse for Chinon, a small towne lying upon the River Vien, here with candles in our hands wee enter'd the contemplative cave of Rabblais which goes under a high hill, with a castle on the top; they say that the English dugg this place to distress the castle, by draining of a well which comes downe into it and causes those drillings of water which then meete withall in the windings of the cave, and at the entrance are received in tanks cutt in the rock: they tell then that this witty Rablais studied here at the Signe of the Lamprey. Leaving this wee passt through Candee a long village, then all along through rows of wallnut-trees, one the one hand the River Loyar, on the other rocks with severall caves and houses in them, continuing till wee arriv'd again at Saumur.

Doiy[116]

A NOTHER EXCURSION WEE made to this old towne which lies upon a wide plain about 4 leagues from Saumur. Hither wee came to view the ruines of an antient amphitheater built in the time of Augustus, and for the most part hew'd out of the rock. It containes 22 steps or seats in heigth, at the farther corner opposite to the entrance was the Emperors seate aloft; the cave of the criminalls, and others for the wilde beasts, all wide and of high arch'd worke. A great fountain in the towne inviron'd with an old wall, whence the water issued for the use of the amphitheater. Wee caresst ourselves here, and retourn'd to Saumur by the evening.

June the first I took horse for Bogee[117] where wee remained all that night, and next day went for –

115   Champigny-sur-Veude.
116   Doue-la-Fontaine?
117   Baugé.

Laflech[118]

TIS BUT A small towne, but pretty neate lying upon a rivulet cal'd La Loire. It is most famous for the great college of Jesuites founded by Henry 4 who was so kinds as to readmitt them, after their expulsion from France.

Here wee were show'd a gallery meanely painted by one of the fathers, wherein were described many great acts of that king. A verry neate apothecaries shop wherein were most sorts of medicinall things kept with great order, and curiosity; the schooles, library, and walkes allso in good order. A magnificent altar in the chappel, with the harts of Henry 4 and Maria de Medici his last Queene sett in wrought worke well guilded. Afterward wee went to the gardens of the Marquess d'Leverin Governour of the towne, but it is a verry indiferent fortification. Hence wee directed our course towards Angiers,[119] and in the way view'd an old chatteau building that did belong to the Duke d'Lyoncore called Durtall. It is a stronge lofty building, but much decayed being rarely inhabited, the garden here was one of the best ordered plats of ground that I have seene lying upon the side of a hill made out into terras's with easie descents to the river side, where runne a pleasant walke of trees of your hornbeame, cutt into severall things like a wall of polite architecture; from this place wee rode to another old seate named Verger belonging to the princess of Gimini mother to that unhappy gentleman Chivalier d'Rhoan beheaded at Paris by this present king; the structure though two hundred yeares standing seemes verry fresh still. At the entrance of the court in a peazo was pourtraide the linage of the family deriv'd from the antient Dukes of Brittaign, a neate chappel with well painted windows. A vast staier case whereon wee might easily ascend eight a brest, the roomes generally darke affording curiosity of guilding and painting with rich roofes. Old furniture, hangings wrought in old characters such as the taking of Hierusalem by Vespasian. It is surrounded with a deepe fosse and for the present uninhabited. About the evening wee reach'd the citty of

Angiers

A BULKIE CITTY, the metropolis of Anjou, and an Episcopall See lying upon the River Mayne.[120] It is circuated with a decayed fortification, and a deepe trench. On the farther side stands an antient chatteau with many tourels built by Reynce titular King of Scicilie, and Hierusalem whose daughter married that inhappy prince Henry 6. Here in a low vault, or dungeon, was a devise verry observable. A small roome standing verry darke, and solitary,

118   La Flèche.
119   Angers; Durtal.
120   River Mayenne.

made like a cage verry stronge with timber, and plates of iron, wherein hee confin'd his Queene for jealousy about the space of thirteene yeers till death came and released her. Over the bridge on the farther side of the towne, stands a poore contemptible building, which is cal'd the pallace of Reynce Duke of Anjou; somwhat higher wee passt over the river in a boate, and went into the Isle of St Obien, a fruitfull spott of land belonging to the Benedictine monkes.

The parts adjacent to this citty are famous for slate-quarrs, from whence Paris is supplied, and most parts of France that way. One of them I take to bee a greate rarity, having been wrought in above 30 yeares, and is upward of 200 foot in depth, and of a mighty extent insomuch that a hundred working at the bottom at a time seeme inconsiderable. It has 4 wells, 3 drain'd by horse, and one by men. On top were severall workmen rending the slate fashioning it into covering.

In the cathedrall which is dedicated to St Morrice wee beheld the tombe of Reynce and his Queene, and here were placed the severall pageants of waxe which were to be used at the next dayes ceremonie cal'd the Sacree which was in this manner: As they stood a long writing was annext to each of them for explanation of the emblem. Here was represented the marriage of Solomon with King Pharaohs daugher, the marriage of Hester, and Ahasuerus, all the nobles and attendance trickt up in the French mode in pantalones, Nathan the prophet rebuking King David for the death of Uriah and defiling his wife. In one of them old Luther was drag'd chain'd to a triumphall charriot driven by an angel; but Calvin made more youthfull and spruse with his hands behind him chain'd to a pillar, both in black gownes; the pageants were about 12 in number all carried on mens shoulders through the streets, most of the rable baring lighted tapers in their hands, the Bourgeois or Magistrates of the towne, the Phisitians, Lawyers, and the several Religious Orders; the Governour the Marquess of Anjou with a white taper unlighted in his hand, all according to their ranke, and order carrying banners with the pictures of saints in them. In one was pourtraide the Holy Virgin a band of miserable violins playing after it with flutes and hoboies. The Host was born under a canopy of state, the Bishop himself being one of the supporters, the Chanonois all in rich capes baring reliques, crosses, and such knacks, so that the ceremonie seem'd more ridiculous than that at Orleans.

Saturday the 12th Instant early in the morning wee took boate for Nantes in Britaigny, by the way wee baited at Ingraunde[121] where wee first entered the province: the Maltoties often troubled our boate with searches, issuing out of huts, and places by the river side. The wind proving contrary wee

121   Ingrandes.

were forced to lodge at a small Aubourge 7 leagues short of the citty, being in all but 17. Wee passt by an old castle apertaining to the Duke of Brisack, the river all along continues full of sands, and islands.

About 11 of the clock next day wee reacht the towne.

Nantes

THIS TOWNE IS populous, well-built, and abounding in trade, the tide comming up hither upon the Loire, by which meanes small vessels are able to ride here, for all the incommoding of the sands of the river which are thick all along. This place is mightily bigotted to the Romish superstition, so that it offers you the sight of many faire churches. St Peters is a lofty building with a carv'd frontispice on which were ingrav'd St Peter, and St Paule; the outside of the gates faced with copper. Wee saw the Capuchions at the upper end whereof stood a shrine of the Virgin with this inscription underneath *Finis Damnationis Maria et origo salutis*. Hence wee went to the Carmes church where wee beheld that goodly tombe erected for Francis the 2nd the last Duke of Brittaigny together with his Duchess both of white marble in their robes spotted with ermin, the supporters of his feete being a lyon hers a grey-hound, resting both upon a large stone of black marble supported by the 4 Virtues exquisitely carv'd one whereof was with a double face representing both old age, and youth upon the same head. It was wrought by that famous artificer Michael Comblis.

Half a league without the towne wee saw the Hermitage, being a small convent scituate upon a rock, with 2 or 3 small gardens to it containing four poor, sad Capuchines; by this stood one of the kings great storehouses containing salt. It was our fortune to bee here at the celebration of the Festivall of St John the Baptist, which was with bonfires throughout the towne, in one of the churches wee saw his head cutt in wood and painted over in a charger, at the end of his beard was a hole to put in doubles and deniers offered to his memory, wee saw the like at Angiers at the Feast of St Peter. The mason d'ville seem'd to bee a good old building here. Wee retourn'd again for Angiers on horseback, and for 2 leagues wee journied through a spatious plaine of meadow; afterwards wee found the cuntry grow verry rocky and uneven, yet abounding with good corn, and vinyards. Wee passt under the stately, and lofty tower of Ouden, which for height and proportion is the best that ever I beheld. Wee lodg'd the first night at Ancenis, and the next day wee came to Angiers againe. Here I had allmost forgotten a stray inscription in latine I mett withall in one of the churches of Nantes under the picture of the Virgin Mary.

Ave Filia Dei Patris
Ave Filis Dei Mater
Ave Sponsa Spiritus Sancti
Ave Totius Trinitatis Templum.

Upon our retourn I saw but litle more than before onely an antient pallace belonging to the bishop of this citty cal'd Vental, half a league without the towne neglected and ruinous and the artifice of blanching of wax.

On the 1 of July I left Angiers and rode along upon the levy (to Saumur) which is a Roman worke of greate industry, being a high banke wall'd on each side with great stone and continuing for the most part to Orleans. The king alows some small matte towards the repair; the rest is at the charges of the country, cause it keeps the water from overflowing the low-lands that lie that way.

July the 5th I departed from Saumur with the Messenger to Rochelle, paying 7 crownes a head; wee made three dayes journey of it. The first night wee lodg'd at Thouars in Poictou, a good towne with an old fortification and a large port at the entrance; here is a noble structure belonging to the family of the Duke d'Tremullie. It is scituate upon a hill close by the towne, the river Thou[122] running under it, but the Messenger going out so early in the morning gave mee no time to see the inside. Wee ferried over the river and mounting the rising on the other side wee had a pretty good sight of this building, which shows verry magnificent, having been all erected within 40 years, being of stone and off a greate heigth: the next night wee lodg'd at Fosses a poore bourge; the next day through Fonteney a large towne, where wee took a small repast, hence to Goy where wee took boate with our horses, and went 2 leagues upon the River Vandy, till wee came to Marans which is at the entrance of the province of Santonge. Poictou continued verry fruitfull all along, with spatious prospects over the vinyards, here and there rocky with stones of a prodigious bignesse. They reckon 30 leagues from Saumur to Rochelle, here I lodg'd at the signe of the *Galliere* upon the Canton de Flemmains the meeting place for the Merchants.

Rochelle

The towne is neate, built for the most part with peatzo's, each side arch't worke. It was formerly noted for the exercise of the protestant religion, but of late years mad[e] a Bishopric occasion'd by the treacherous dealings they received from England under Charles the first, who overrul'd by his French wife suffer'd them to be distresst for want of timely reliefe; so that they were forced to yield to the mercy of Luis the 13th and his great Cardinall Richlieu, who having reduct them raz'd their walls, and constrain'd them to admitt of Episcopacy and the Catholick religion againe: but for all this the number of the Hugonotes is greate here, being allow'd a Temple a litle without the towne. The cathedrall of the citty was formerly the Grand Temple a faire ovall building, a large space of ground lying by it, which leades up to house of the Capuchines used for promanading. Here they show'd us the reliques of port St Luis, from whence the batteries were made upon the towne. They (sic) ships lie here very commodious before the Key, 2 old Forts standing to guard the entrance, and a chaine drawne athwart every night to keepe um from going out or in without orders. Here are some remnants of the Dique [dike] which the Cardinal caused to be cast up for the transporting of horse to the island, and hindering of ships from bringing in relief to the towne during the siege.

And on the 12th Instant wee took horse and rode to the ferry, and so sail'd over to the Isle of –

Rhee[123]

THE ISLAND IS but small, sandy, and barren yet by the industry of the inhabitants, it brings in a considerable proffit to the Crowne it producing yearly three hundred thousand quarters of salt, and 50000 tunne of wine. Just upon our landing wee saw a strong fort which the trecherous, courtly Duke of Buckingham slighted at his comming here. Upon our landing, the boyes and girles stood ready with horses of hire on which wee mounted, and wrode through La Flota, and so to St Martins the capitol of the Isle; wee found scarse any thing observable in this place, only a Dock for ships, and a poore house of Capuchins. Wee retourned again on foot to the vessel, and after landing tooke horse againe, and by night came to Rochelle.

July the 27th I took Messenger from hence to Bourdeaux paying 12 crownes for mee and my man, the first night I lodg'd at –

Rochfort[124]

THIS IS A new built towne, but as yet imperfect lying like a heape of rubbish. It stands upon the River Charant in which commonly ly 30 or 40 good men of warr, the tide flowing up a good way into the cuntry. The place was design'd for the accommodating shiping that may bee ready for the guarding these parts that lie towards the Brittish seas. The kings storehouses for

123   Ile de Ré; La Flotte; St Martin.
124   Rochefort; River Chardente;

these navall preparations lie all upon the banke of this river being new-built, and of a compleate model. First the Corderie, the place in which the cabels are made, being of a very great length and a hansome building; the roome over it was for making of twine for supplying the same. Then the Arsenall wherein are the storehouses for each particular ship belonging to the place, with the names of them wrote over the doores in letters of gold. Then the magazine of swords, pikes, and musquets which were kept very cleane, and in great order. The powderhouse, and the severall places for making of anchors and all sorts of iron worke for ships, compleate and in singular good order. Wee went hence and dined the next day at –

Saintes

T HIS IS AN antient towne and the metropolis of Santonge. Here is a verry antique church consecrated to St Eutrope, you descend severall steps into a vault where are many altars, comming up again you have 2 ascents that leade you into the upper church over this vault, where in the wall at the High Altar stands the head of St Eutrope in silver with a litle mantle wrapt about it, and an iron grate before it; 'tis said it was built by the English. Hard by this wee wee went to see the ruines of a large amphitheater of an ovall figure (but greatly decayed) in which was a fountain dedicated to Sainte Eustelle whose picture was hung up in the arch for devotion sake; then wee went to an old demolisht fort upon a hill, which gave us the sight of the towne; and so to the old long bridge with severall gates reaching over the Charant. Wee reacht Pons this night, a large towne, where wee lodg'd, and the next day wee dine'd at Petit-Nort, thence to Blay to bed where stands an old fort with a garrison to secure the comming into the Garrone. In the morning about three of the clock wee tooke boate here and went up the same river, having left the province of Santonge, which seem'd a pleasant cuntry throughout, yet more stony and barren than Poictou, and not so abounding with vinyards and large prospects. By seven of the clock wee toucht at the citty of

Bourdeaux[125]

H ERE I TOOK up my lodging at the *Shappoe Rouge*. The Sunday after I arriv'd wee went to Beglee where wee saw a great confluxof Hugonotes; here wee din'd, went to church, in the afternoone and retourned by boate again. After this wee saw the Temple of the Tutelar Gods erected by Julius Cesar, there still remaine 17 lofty columes with Corinthian capitols, and statues over each but so decay'd by antiquity that there is litle of form to bee

125   Bordeaux; Chapeau Rouge? Bègles.

discern'd. Underneath is a great arch of stone. It serves now for a Taverne.

Afterwards to the Chatteau Trumpet which is a compleat building consisting of 6 bastions showing much of strength, and beauty, but not yet quite finished, the batteries were but indifferently gun'd, but very neate, and artificiall, the walls rail'd about with iron worke in the manner of balconies. Adjoining to this toward the towne was a half-moone newly erected; but being upon spungy ground prov'd verry unwholsome to the souldiers and noysomm by the setlement of the fosse.

Now to the amphitheater lying a small distance from the towne by some cal'd Palais Galiene, where wee beheld a noble wide ruine with 2 lofty gates opposite to each other, the highway leading through it; a litle beyond this is a faire fountaine erected at the charge of the Sexemviri or Jurats of the towne. Then wee saw the Town-house, wherein were the pictures of many old Jurats, the severall measures of things cast in iron; at the entrance stood 3 old Roman figures in neeches viz: Claudius, ?Drusus and Messilina, the 2 men had their heads broken off, but the woman an entire delicate figure.

On Thursday being the day that they open wee went to see the Carthusians who had a most delightfull chappel, they are a rich convent eonsisting of 24 in number all in white habit. Then wee went to the cathedrall church of St Andrews to heare vespers, the Arch-bishop officiated it being a solemne day; here wee observ'd the manner of their sitting, those of the parlament of Bourdeaux were in scarlet gownes, the Jurates sate next to um in gownes one side white and t'other purple. Through the towne in the evening they went procession with a great rable. Next wee saw the church of St Michael, and mounted the tower to take a prospect of the towne. Another day for our diversion wee row'd up the water to Cadillac (5 leagues distant) to view a stately structure raised by the great Duke of Espernon; the roomes are large and lofty, many costly carv'd chimney pieces; the furniture but litle by reason of a litigious controversie about the title. Here were the acts of the great Gaston d'Foy from whome the Duke descended, rich guilded roofes and rafters, a lofty chapel well painted; wee saw likewise many rich copes, and presents made to the church and chanons in the towne. All the offices of arch't worke, under ground, large, and capacious. The gardens, and grotts decayed but the Mal the longest and most pleasant that I saw in all the country lying pleasantly on the side of the Garrone.

During our abode here we saw a mutiny of the people upon the bringing in of the Papier-Timbrie, which is a new imposition, which they say they ought to bee freed from, by contract from their former kings for helping to expell the English out of Guiene, but this tumult was quickly over, and many of the actors in it punisht with death. The towne is very populous and compleatly built, the Shappoe-Rouge Street being as spatious as any throughout France.

On the 8th of August I left this place, and lodg'd the first night at Cadilliac.[126] Hence I took horse early in the morning, of the Voiturier, or post paying 24 crownes for mee and my Man for all accommodation betweene this and Thoulouse;[127] we rode 4 stages in the morning and then din'd at Marmande passing through Agen (fam'd for the birth of Julius Scaliger) and the cuntry of Agenois. The product of these parts upon the side of the Garonne is generally hempe. We saw many hills with ruin'd chatteaus on the top. Wee lodg'd at Maistate[128] in the same province this night having wrod 4 stages more; the next morning wee wrode 5 more going through part of Gascogne, which abounds allso with hempe, but few vinyards, many great mountains lying on our right hand.

The villages exceeding poore, encompass't with mud-walls; though the houses generally are of brick yet show verry antique. For the conveniency of the Courrier in delivering his letters we were forc't to ferry over diverse streams and rivers; at length wee enter'd the delightfull cuntry of Languedoc and about midday came to the famous citty of –

Thoulouse[129]

THIS TOWNE IS exceeding large, and the capitol of Languedoc, built generally of brick, with some paper buildings verry antient all coverd with pantile, large eves jetting out from the top to shade the streetes from the violent heates. I lodg'd at Ville d'Alby at one Monsieur d'Shotes neere the Place St Estiene paying a crowne a day for mee and my Man. First of all wee went to view the Capitol or Townehouse being a large building of brick in which are severall spatious roomes for Justice painted with the Octumviri in their robes, which are the Magistrates of the citty, as this Sexemviri at Bourdeaux. Here in the anticourt before the frontispiece of the house they show'd us where the Duke d'Montmorancy was beheaded, some of the sprinklings of the blood being yet apparent on the wall. In one of the roomes where they sitt for determining causes I found this inscription *Videant Senatores ne quid detrimenti Respublica capiat*. In a great upper rome wee saw the busto's of some Men of Note that received their birth in the towne viz: Antonius 1 Emperor of Rome, Theodorick King of the Thoulouse, and L: Statius professor of Rhetorick in

126 Cadillac (as previously).
127 Toulouse.
128 Maistate?
129 Toulouse.

this place; then the rome where the towne magazine lay.

After this wee went to see the Chatteau Moulin, which are many water mills, in an old brick-building like a Fort. Wee saw a stately bridge of brick built over the Garonne in the infancie of this king as appears by an inscription in Latin verse over a large port at the farther end with lofty pavilions; the old one had been ruin'd by the floods; as you may see by the remnant of one arch yet in beeing. Wee went to the palais the place wherein the parlaments are held, and all the Law-Courts kept, this being one of the greatest nurseries for lawyers in France. The chappel of the penitent noir here is but a meane building, but the inside is highly illustrated with guilding, carving, and painting wherein the batles of Constantine were expresst. At the church of the Pere Professe, wee saw a tombe of black marble wherein the hart of the great Montmorancy was enshrin'd.

Now to the church of St Sermine which is strongly built and serves this citty instead of a Fortresse, being planted with gunns over the arch at coming in. We saw many goodly rich altars but the principall rarities were in the vault under the Quier, viz: costly shrines, and reliques, the harts of 7 of the Apostles and many of their heads enchas't in silver. The head of an old English king whome they call St Emon. I know not whether they meane Edmund or old Simon the King one as likely as the other in my judgment; then wee saw the head of the faire Susannæ so tradu'd by the Elders. One of the stones that were throwne at St Stephen when he sufferd martyrdome, about the bigness of both of my fists inclosed in a silver case. The church of the Cordeliers was painted with the history of St Francis, where he rebukes the Frier that thought hee had found a Money-bagg, and being greedy to open it let the Devil out of it. Wee saw the mighty altar in the Jacobines church, and the grand and petit Augustines. Wee mounted the tower of St Etiene to take the prospect of the towne and see the great bell cal'd Cadillac, which I take to bee bigger than that at Tours.

In the forementioned church of the Cordeliers I had allmost forgotten one of the greatest rarities that ever I mett withall, which was the drie bodies standing about the cave under the Quier, in various postures, the earth being of that heating quality, that in 2 or 3 yeares space it dries them of the colour of mumie, only not so hardned (sic). Here wee beheld part of the corps of Bellepaule from the twist downwards, a Lady once verry renown'd for beauty, and much talk't of by travellers but they have so peel'd her skinne away that there is litle remaining but the bare-bones. At the upper end of the vault stood an woodden Cross, and the bodies of some small children dryed in this manner.

On the 15th Instant being Sunday I hir'd 3 horses, and give 15 crownes for defraying all charges betweene this and Monpelier.[130] I rode along the side of the Canal Royall. Presently after I came out of Thoulouse and so continued till I came to dine at Vilnovelle; toward the evening I came in view of the Grand-Basin at Narouse with the Rigolle and severall sluces, and the mill. It is an octogon of a vast circumference but at this time not quite finisht. About night wee came to lodge at the old citty of Castelnaudari,[131] a Bishoprick, yet a poorre raggid place allmost as meane as Peterburrow in Northamptonshire. The next day wee dined at Carcassone,[132] both the upper and lower towne seeming to bee well fortified considering the antiquity thereof. Here we came in sight of the haughty Pyreneans on the right hand, and on the other side stood the black mountains. This night wee lodg'd at Pechiri; the way stony and many mountanous ascents, here and there a few olive trees. The next day wee dined at Pont d'Cavasic, and so to lodge at Bessiers,[133] an old fortified citty, and a Bishoprick, here were many Spanish prisoners kept that had been taken by Count Shambourge. Now wee begann to pass through very pleasant vallies of olives in which the flying grasshoppers made a pretty kind of noyes, and ever and anon hedges of tamariske, and pomgranade trees. Here I beganne to find the Canal quite dry and the cut discontinued in some places. The last day wee din'd at Loupian and so to Montpelier.[134]

Montpelier

THIS TOWNE HAS a pleasant scituation, in an odorous fragrant aier, within 2 leagues of the Mediterranean sea. It is incompass'd with an old wall. Without the towne is a new-built citadel of no great validity; tis an episcopall see but the cathedrall, meane and ruinous by the Hugonotes meanes as they say; the place is principally noted for restoring, consumptive decayed bodies, and for the professors of phisick, which resort here by reason of the variety of herbs and simples that grow in these parts; and the taking their degrees. Here is laide the designe of a noble phisick-garden, which they call L'Jardin-du-Roy, but tis as yet unfinisht. The Canourge or place where the ladies, and gallants walke is but small, being only a plot of ground formerly design'd for a church, nor indeede ha's the towne any diversion, or observable antiquity in it. About the midle of the towne under the effigies of the Virgin Mary were these 2 verses

130   Later, Walker spells this name Montpelier. Canal du Midi; Castelnaudary;
131   Castelnaudary
132   Carcassonne.
133   Béziers.
134   Montpellier.

Virgo tuare fidem, virgo defende fideles
Marspelium virgo sit tibi palladium.

Here are abundance of perfumes, and esssences made and the Alcermis a
little red berry so noted for perfumes, and cordialls grows here. Sunday the
22nd wee tooke horse, and went through an odorous cuntry all the way, with
vinyards of Frontignian[135] and at last came to Port Louis, or

Cape-Cotte

THIS IS FIVE leagues distant from Monpelier. Here wee behld a costly, and
mighty worke the Mould (for securing of ships that ride there) which
runns about a thousand paces into the sea, and is neere 20 yards in breadth, all
of stone with severall descents to the ships and great pillar'd stones to fix their
cables at; one end of the canal comes downe to this part to receive the traffick
of the Mediterranean to bee carried through Languedoc in boates. As yet here
are onely some few houses built on the side of the hill for the accommodation
of those that worke on the Mould, so that wee could have no conveniency
here, but were forc't to retourn and dine at the litle towne of Frontignian,
which gives the name to that delicious wine made of the Muscat grapes, and so
by night to Monpelier again.

August the 23. I hir'd the voiturier for 2 crownes a day with 2 horses in
order to the making the tour of Provence. The first day wee travelled through
a fragrant cuntry breathing the sweete odours of myrh, and lavander, through
groves of juniper and mulberries, and came that night to lodge at the old citty
of Arles in this province.

Arles

IT IS WELL seated on the bankes of the River Rhone which wee passt over
upon a bridge of boates to enter the towne. The streetes are narrow, the
houses old, and not verry well-built: yet here wee found many noble antiquities.
First I tooke a Guide who conducted mee to the Town-House, where I saw
2 old statues the one of Jupiter, 'tother of Diana which was incomparably
carv'd, and very beautifull being all entire except the right arme; the Goddess
is carv'd naked downe to the midle, the lower parts habited in the manner of
the Roman matrons, her feete and leggs appearing a litle above the ankles; she
stood leaning forward in a posture as if she were delivering her oracles to the
people. She was made somwhat higher of proportion than usually the life, on
the top of her forehead was a small hole in which they suppose was fastned a

135   Of Frontignan.

christall, or a silver crescent. She was dugg out of the ruines of her owne temple (upon sinking of a well) whereof are many remnants scatter'd up and downe here, and there they say that Sanctus Trophimus preaching Christianity here wrought so effectually upon the people, that they immediately destroyed their owne temple wherein this beauteous goddess was worshipped.

In one place wee saw 2 lofty columnes standing with Corinthian capitols, and an arch over them; a large altar stone of white marble with a well-wrought freeze; many broken pieces of columes. A gate of this temple with a cornish carv'd with the figures of bulls, staggs, and ramms, and such horned beasts as were usually offer'd to the goddess for sacrifice. Tis reported that they annually immolated 2 young children to her. Another port standing even with the wall of the towne toward the river, which is cal'd the Gate of Rowland. And in a garden just without the towne is an extreme large stone, great part sunke into the earth, which is said to bee the altar stone on which they laide their beast offerings, which has given the name of Ara Sata to the towne. In the kitchen of an apothecaries house wee were afterwards show'd the body of Laocaon the priest of Phæbus (dugg out of the ruines) which was by a prodigie destroyed at Troy (for running his speare at the Trojan Horse) by 2 serpents that came out of the river and infolded him which were admirably expresst in the carv'd worke the signes of the Zodiack being intermixt in the folds. It was cal'd by some L'Dieu d'Battaile. The next was the Arhenes, or ruines of an amphitheater built by Severus; this was a very large one, one of the gates still remaining entire; but the rest so clog'd with building that 'tis a hard matter to take a good accompt of it. The vaults remain still intire.

About midday wee left this place, and neere a quarter of a league out of the towne wee found the tombs of abundance of old Romans that had been slaine in the fields of ?Catreume, in a place cal'd the Elizium Fields many inscriptions on them, and verry great stones but in those that lay open nought but durt and rubbish. Hence wee went on to the house of the Friers Minims where wee saw an old chappel, with much carving in marble (in relieve) of the history of Scripture; then under the conduct of a frier wee descended into a vault to see the tombs of many antient bishops of Arles, together with the tombe of Rowland whose hunting-horn wee had seen at Thoulouse. I remember at the half-space about the midle of the staier case of this religieuse house was fixt a stone with a Romane inscription D.M. and Domitianus plainly read. As wee came into the gallery at the farther end wee saw a monstrous deformed kind of picture drawne upon the wall in large proportion, drawing somwhat nearer the frier directed us to stand still, and looke againe and then wee found it contracted to the proportiom of a comly young man sitting on an eagle, and

gazing upwards; which it seems was the embleme of St John the Evangelist.
We travel'd for the remaining part of this day through a wild cuntry with
mountanous rocks, and came to Salone which lies as if you were to drop into't
from the rocks.

Salone[136]

NOTHING HERE VERY remarkable but the tombe of Nostredamus that
fam'd astrologer. It is in the old chappel of the Cordeliers, a stone sett into
the side of the wall on the left hand as you enter the chappel, giving an accompt
that hee had *Incredibilem Astrorum Scientiam*. He lived 62 years, and dyed Anno
1566. Leaving this towne wee continued still in a rocky cuntry, wee had a very
terrible access by winding wayes hew'd out of a rock to pass through a village
cal'd La Peine which was plac'd on the top thereof. Wee wrode through many
groves of almond trees and came now in view of the bastites or multitude of litle
cottages that are built for the guard of the vinyards about Marselles.

Marselles

WEE IMMEDIATELY ENTER'D here into a streete of sumptuous building
and lodg'd at the Signe of the *Teste-noir*; at the upper part of this
streete stood the Arsenall which is stately built, and commodious for all navall
accommodation. In the first court wee saw 2 noble docks for building of gallyes
with (sic) coverings over head, in one whereof they were making a large galley.
Neere these coverings, or penthouses are two side walkes of broadstone resting
upon arches of the same, under which they have the conveniency of working
their timber though in fowle weather. In the farther court were the sawyers and
other meaner artificers. In a long entry under a side building lay severall piles of
oars some for 3 other for four slaves apiece being neere 35 foot in length. This
building opens most stately toward the harbour, with a lofty front and 2 pavilions
on each side. The harbour is but smalle, yet delicate to the view, inviron'd with
many curious buildings, as the Mason d'Ville with goodly colummes of marble
and carv'd worke on the front, with a large Key, the Arsenall, chatteau and many
good houses adorning it. The entrance of the port is commanded by a fort on
the left hand, and a Cittadel on the right which I could bee permitted to enter
as a stranger. Here wee saw the brave Gally-Royall in harbour, containing 300
slave, 2 gallies more lying by her, and 2 galliots. I left this place the next day after
dinner, and wrode over the Mountaine St Jean, being a great rock on the highest
point whereof stood a poore hermits cell, part whereof was hew'd out of the rock;
the access to it mighty steepe, and difficult. In our way wee saw a multitide of

136   Salon-de-Provence.

pines bleeding turpentine, an abundance of odorous sweete herbes, and so came to lodge at Sante-bome.[137]

Sancte-Bome

WEE CLAMBER'D UP an exceeding steepe rock for the space of above an houre to come to this place where wee lodg'd (which was but half-way to the top of the rock). Here is a co[n]vent of some 6 or 7 Friers in a white habit that are devoted to the Holy-Sinner Mary Magdalene; they have a litle building to entertaine passengers, with stables hew'd out of the rock for the mules, and horses, adjoining to the religious house. From the convent ascending some 12 steps you enter a large cave which is made use of as a chappell for this sainte, no light but what is intromitted from the doore. Only at the upper end was a sacell inclosed with iron grates wherein lay the effigies of this faire saint resting upon her elbow, and leaning against a small artificiall rocke, with many lamps of silver burning about her, an altar at her head where the votaries kneele dayly. At the farther end is a spring of pure water drilling from the rock; wee descended nigh 20 steps from this upper chappell into a vault, wherein an altar stood obscurely, carv'd with the dolefull spectacle of our Saviours being lamented in the Sepulcher.

The next morning being Sunday the place was mightily frequented by abundance of superstitious votaries (especially women) who haunt this shrine in hopes of being forgiven this delightfull sinne. Standing at the shrine I saw many of them earnestly pressing to kisse the faire sainte as they cal'd her. Aboute eleven of the clock wee left this place, and mounted on foot to the brow of the rock, which lies about a mile higher, from which you have a wonderfull prospect into the valley, the olive-trees appearing not above a yard-high; on the highest part stood a small chappel with a cupola (cal'd St Pilon[138]) wherein was carv'd a fair Magdalene standing on the altar all naked; her hair loosely flowing, and waving about her belly; an iron dore at the entrance made open like a grate, through which they might behold the sainte, and throw in their offerings of doubles, and other small money. Hence we wrode for a long way through the clefts of the rocks, and by the evening came to –

Toulone[139]

THIS TOWNE IS but ordinary building, and much less than Marselles; it is so closely environ'd with hills, that it renders it intolerably hott,

---

137 Sainte Baume.

138 Marked as a tourist attraction on a modern map of France.

139 Toulon.

and inconvenient to strangers; but it is conveniently scituated one this side of a spatious harbour, being about 40 foot in depth, a large Key likewise for the landing of goods. The harbour is divided by the Mole into two parts, for the rendring the inner part more secure: this Mole is a vast worke well mounted with gunns and a fort for farther safeguard. The outward harbour ha's 2 opposite Forts to guard the entrance from the Mediterranean. In the inner port lay severall great vessels viz: the guilded-Grand-Louis 2000 tunne in burden, and bares 120 gunns, then la Reyne, L'Douphin and the Grand-Monarque wherein I was abord, she bares 110 gunns. Wee saw no gallies at all here. Many small ships were loosing from hence to carry relief to Messina.

Then wee went to the Arsenall which is larger but so well-built as that at Marselles, it is so large that it usually containes 4000 men at a time at worke. In a long gallery on one of the courts were nigh 1000 women at worke for making of sailes. In another were the carpenters, and joyners. Upon one of the carv'd prows of a ship wee saw this haughty motto

Quo Jussa Tonantis

Then wee came to the vaulted chambers of stone-worke where the tarponds were for dipping of cables. From hence being but 3 leagues wee went to lodge at –

Yeres[140]

THIS IS AN extreme pleasant village, full of orangeries; the gardens here are very large and numerous, and afford litle else but this kind of frute, vast quantities of oranges of China, Valence, large citrons, the boughs so laden that they are forc'd to support them with forkes, the trees being neere as large as apple-trees with us. Between the rows of this fruite are generally beds of fragrant Spannish jessemin, and against the walls rows of cassia trees; with trenches for small currents of water betweee the ranks; the blasts of aier seeme fragrant even to a wonder. On the morrow in the morning wee went hence travelling for 6 league through a rocky cuntry till wee came to

St Maximin[141]

THIS IS MOST remarkable for the great co[n]vent of friers founded here by Carolus Claudus king of France who having been held in durance for a long time in Spaine, was at last upon the fervency of his prayers releast by an angel, who took him up, and sett him downe in this part of Provence. It is a

140   Hyères.
141   St Maximin-le-Ste Baume,

large church consisting of a large number of friers in a white habit. In a vault in this church is preserv'd the scull of Mary Magdalene in a christall enchas'd with silver verry massif, and rich; likewise her tombe close by it. In another part of the church wee were show'd the haire wherewith she wip'd our Saviours feete, and other such reliques. I was conducted into the library by an Irish frier, who as a choise rarity show'd mee that memorable booke cal'd Εἰκὼν Βασιλική. The next day through rocks being 6 leagues to Aix

Aix

THIS I FOUND a pleasant, beautifull citty lying upon gently rising ground; tis the metropolis of Provence, the place in which the parlaments are held; the palais in which they sitt is an antient building, and the cathedral but ordinary, but the Bel-Cour, or large streete going downe to the old walls of the towne is the fairest that ever I saw, sett with 4 rows of trees, and a most stately range of building on the left hand, but not quite finisht; the structure on the right hand does not so well correspond with it. Here are naturall hott baths in this towne, so that it was cal'd by the Romans Aqua Sextii.

Wee went onward of our jounrey travelling 8 leagues, and came at night to Ourgon a small village lying under the rocks on this side of the rapid river of Durance; the next day wee din'd at Tarascone an old towne where they show you the sepulcher of Martha sister of Mary Magdalene; this was the last towne wee saw in Provence;[142] wee ferried over the Rhone to Boqueros[143] and came that night to Niemes still remaining in a rocky cuntry but not so bad as before, and the next day to Monpelier againe. This journey stood me in 6 Luis-d'ors. Here I remained about a weeke longer, and on the 11th of 7br [September] hir'd a voiturier and 3 horses giving eight Luis d'ors for 9 dayes, nourishment included, and for the seeing the principall antiquities, and things of note in the way; wee din'd at Pont d'Lunel and that evening came to Niemes.[144]

Niemes

THIS IS CERTAINLY a towne of the most antiquity of any throughout France, some say it was founded by Nemansus the son of Hercules; and was afterwards a famous Roman colony, but raz'd by Charles Martel, and not restor'd again out of its ruines for many yeares. The chiefest thing here is that goodly vast building the amphitheater, which as yet remaines pretty entire considering the long time, and neglect it has undergone. The upper

142   Orgon; Tarascon.
143   Beaucaire.
144   Nimes.

arches remaine so well that they afford a passage quite round; in this circuit wee were show'd 2 stones that the fabulous people say were laide by the 2 brothers Romulus, and Remus. The lower arches are fil'd up and obstructed with building and so are the arrhenes. The seats for the vulgar give a stately view from side to side. The entrance to the Imperial seate is made more stately <noble> than the rest in the upper row of arches, being an architrave supported by 2 columes, with 2 great bulls-heads carv'd at the corners, which is cal'd the Tauro's. Just over the lower arches, wee saw diverse carv'd works upon the wall viz: 2 gladiators combating Romulus and Remus sucking the wolfe; and 3 grand genitals triangularly growing out of one another mounted upon staggs feete with eagles winges, an old woman straining the raines in their mouthes, or ribs with one hand, and furiously lashing them with the other, which some imagine to bee the embleme of revenge for the Romans ravishing the Sabinian girles. In the midle of the arrhenes stood a large fountaine fedd by that mighty Acqueduct at Pont du Guard. Wee enter'd 2 of their caves where they kept their lyons, and wild beasts. The figure of the building is ovall, all of vast well-polisht stone, yet not all of the same manner of worke, as appeares by the cornish, and basis of some of the arches. In other parts of the towne wee saw abundance of Roman inscriptions; many tombstones dedicated
dedicated] D.M. *Divis Manibus*.

In the courts of many of the gentlemens houses wee ever now and then mett with carv'd workes as an hippotomus with this motto *Procul este prophani*; then a boy flying up a globe but hindred by the Æquinoctiall line with this underwritten *Trabs huius Mundi impedit volare ad Beatitudinem*, the quatre-jambe which is a rude image without a head, resting upon four leggs. Many remaines of vast columes in white marble of the Corinthian lying about the streetes. Wee now went on to the Mason-Quarrie the most stately thing for the bigness that ever I mett withall, 'tis supported by 30 marble pillars of the Corinthian order, frise, and cornish the same, with a spatious portall, the space betweene these columes is now fil'd up with small stones, and us'd as an habitation for some poore people; the doore from the portall seems to have been very ample, and magnificant; wee enter'd and took a farther view of the columnes in the inside by which meanes wee were better able to see the carving of their capitals which show'd great curiosity, and scarse to bee match't in these dayes; some say it was created by Trajan as a pallace for his Empress; others that it was a pleading house for hearing and determining causes. In many places wee saw the carv'd heads of the Roman Eagles cutt off, which was donne by the spight and malice of the Goths invading Italy this way.

After this wee went to the farther end of the towne to see the noble ruines of the Temple of Diana, great part of the arch'd worke yet remaining, likewise the vast arches for the altars, and the statue of the goddesse; the wall on the right side is yet entire, with neeches in it, parted with plaine columes with Corinthian capitols. There remaines as yet a side isle cover'd over, through which they brought in the catle for sacrifice. Without this stands the fountain of the goddess inviron'd with an old wall, tis fabulously reported this water ha's no bottom. Some say it was the temple of Serapis, and that the priest did annually drowne the god in this well, which was onely a speckl'd heifer. Certain it is that the people of most of these townes give but a defective accompt of their antiquities. The bishop of this citty (as a hater of idolatry) caus'd severall stones to bee taken from this temple, and brought to his palace for the erecting of gates, and ornaments for his house, and gardens, but was at last forbidden by the king to make any farther defenestration thereof. This place abounds with Hugonotes and here they have a very neate temple for devotion.

Without the towne wee were conducted to the Tour-Romane which is a solid tower, and part of the old Romane wall which circuited this citty, which with some scattering ruines is a demonstration of its large extent. Here in the rocks wee were diverted with eccho and show'd the quarrie whence the Romans dugge the stones for raising their vast structures. The cursoriness of my notes had allmost caus'd mee to omitt, some rarities wee saw in the cabinet of Monsieur Girane a civilian in this citty, who had been so diligent, and studious as to have wrote a treatise in latine of the antiquities of this place, but not as yet committed to the presse. Hee show'd us an antique head of Jupiter-Hamon with rams-horns carv'd on it. An antient Mercury standing upon an altar. The Ægyptian Anubis. Severall small urnes. A strigil or sort of instrument which they us'd to scrape the bathers withall. A naulus or small piece of money which they put into the mouth of the defunct to pay Charon for ferrying over Styx. Here wee remained till the 12th of 7br [September] and then took our journey toward –

Pont-du-Guard[145]

WHICH IS A lofty stupendous bridge reaching from the brow of one mountain, to another cross the River Guard, 'tis an old Roman worke but by whome erected uncertaine. It is composed of wrought stone of a mighty proportion, and 3 rows of arches standing one upon another, and rising neere 200 foot in heigth. The first row of arches are of a great extent, and thickness; and serves for the conveniency of horse, and foot passsengers, supporting the 2nd row which are large too, upon which rests the third row of smaller arches

145   Pont de Gard.

over which the current of the aquæduct passt through a deepe bed, or canal of small stones flag'd with great ones, and so discharg'd it self into the valley leading to Niemes; some more ruines of arches are yet to bee seene in the valley. The top of this aquæduct is cover'd with broadstone capacious enough to walk on; affording a curious prospect and a delightfull eccho, which did reverberate the sound thrise very distinctly from once speaking. After wee came downe sitting on horseback at some distance and looking through the arches, it represented to us a goodly landskips of hills and forrest worke. After some hours admiration of this stately heape wee went to lodge that night at –

Avignion[146]

THIS IS A citty, and principality about 12 Miles in extent round about, belonging to his Holiness in the province of Venaissin which is the territorie of the king of France. It lies on the bankes of the River Rhone. Just upon our comming on the bridge wee were searcht by the king of France his officers, who are very strict in those matters with all passengers that are strangers; being dismisst from the searches wee went on upon the bridge which wee found much ruined by the impetuosity of the river, so that wee were forced to ferry over part of it in a boate. The vulgar fable that all this bridge was built in three dayes by a poore shepherd, whome they have fondly made a saint of, and sett his statue upp upon the shore.

The towne seemes to be built about a hill, and is girt with an extraordinary good old wall. On top of the hill neere the center of the towne stands a vast castle which is the Popes Pallace in which a Legate, or Vice-Legate has his residence; tis in many places much decayed. First wee were show'd here the Vice-Legates apartment which lay all on on a flore, and indifferently well-furnisht, many wide old roomes, and chappels, amongst which the greate open hall where one of the villanous popes blew up a greate number of the nobless, and gentry in revenge of his nephews death whome they caused to bee hanged at the pallace-gate. In this chappel wee saw 2 or 3 lofty tombs erected for popes interred here. Abundance of fair churches and religious houses in this towne; as the large roofe of the chappel of the Cordeliers without any prop in which is the tomb of the Cardinal of Amboys, St Martian, and Petrachs celebrated Laura. The famous cloyster of the Celestines founded by Charles the 6th of France. Then the rich altar in the Jacobines church. The Jews are here by toleration from his Holiness, and are distinguisht by their waring of yellow hats and are permitted to exercise their religion in a poore synagogue here. All the popes Guard here are in a particolor'd habit half read, and half yellow. The people here pay no taxes but for the keeping of a small horse-guard so that they generally thanke God they are not under the French king.

From hence we wrode away to a litle village cal'd Vocluse a place noted for the retirement of that famous Italian poet Petrach, who here in verse celebrated his much admired Laura. Here wee clamber'd along the rocks and came to a hole at the farther end like a cave, which they say is not to bee fathom'd for the depth of water which breakes out so violently in the winter time, that it resembles a great cascade; wee lodg'd this night at Lisle another towne under the papall jurisdiction and the next day for –

Orange

IN COMMING HITHER wee passt through vallies of mulberries and olives; but the latter not so large as I mett withall in Provence and Languedoc. This citty is but small but verry antient, seated in a rich valley, lying in the cuntry of Venaissin as wells as Avignion. The remnants of antiquities that are still here, show that it was in great estimation by the Romans. The wall of the Cirque shows it to have been a vast and haughty building, 2 old towers standing at each end in which the officers lod'g that were judges of those recreations. On the one side is the open space where they us'd to runne their charriots, and horses; on the other side under the hill was the theater whereon they acted their playes and had their fights and combats represented. Next (which is a sufficient remarque of Roman glory) stands that beautifull, and incomparable worke, the triumphall arch (a litle without the towne) erected in honour of Casius Marius for a great victory obtained over the Cimbri upon the bankes of Rhodanus; the name of his fellow consul (Cajus Catullus) likewise ingraven. Three arches, or ports of passage through, the middle one very spatious, and all adorn'd with an exquisite freese over each arch. The worke is in relievo emblematically figur'd showing many trophies of warr; as Rome sitting in a triumphall charriot in a matrons garbe with the solar beames about her head; driving over the necks of captiv'd king. Cyene the pythonist whome Marius fondly carried about with him to predict the events of batles. Wee went up into the roome of the arch (which was excellently carv'd in flowerd-worke) and inhabited by a poore old man and's wife, much like Baucis and Philemon in the poet; who sold us some old meddalls, and a litle booke of the description of the antiquities of Orange. Great part of the worke is obscured by the butteresses built by one of the princes of Orange to support it against any farther ruine, or decay.

Wee now mounted the hill to see the ruines of a stronge and stately castle belonging to the princes of Orange, but demolisht by the French kings order in the beginning of the warr with Holland. At the bottome of the hill under a ruin'd out tower is a spring which they call Font-Lave-Cone. Afterwards in the towne wee were show'd an antique pavement of mosaick worke downe in a cellar being the figure of a cat in a border of various lively colours.

The next day wee journeyed on to St Esprit[147] continuing still in Venaissin, at the entring this towne wee wrode over a wonderfull bridge both for length, and haughtiness the like I suppose not to bee mett withall throughout France and so wee lodg'd at Montelimart a great towne in Dauphiny, and the next night at Valence upon the River Lisece in the same provence, where in the cloyster of the Jacobines wee saw the skeleton of a giant (15 cubits high) painted on the wall, with the history of his being slaine by a French Count; a romantick litle frier of the Order pretended to show us one of the bones of his left legg; but instead of that brought us the shoulder bone of an ox; such is the delusion of these clergy-men that they can hardly speake truth though in the smallest concernes. The night following we went to Opiage[148] and so to Vienne in Viennois, which had been a noted Roman colony lying upon the Rhone; wee see a faire church here dedicated to St Maurice at the port by it a large stone sett in the wall, ingraven in large letters with a dedication to Hercules, and Mercury. I remember upon our entrance into this towne in a plow'd field, wee beheld a lofty pyramid resting upon a square arch of large stone, exactly corresponding on all sides, which wee judg'd to bee some monument of Roman grandure.

We now left the cuntry of Dauphiny which was for the most part hilly, the ground barren, producing great quantities of the seede which they call Miel-Noir, and great numbers of chestnutts, and on this day being the 18th of 7br [September] wee enter'd Lyonois and so came to the great citty of Lyons.

Lyons

I S A MIGHTY populous large citty, flourishing in trade, and for the most part lying under the covert of lofty hills, on the other side opening into a goodly wide plaine; in which the fierce fight hapned betweene Severus, and Albinus. Here meete two famous rivers (Aroris, and Rhodanus, the Saone and the Rhone) and make their current through a considerable part of this citty; the latter flows out of the Lake of Geneve; these 2 streames meeting here render it somthing an unwholsome scituation caus'd by the foggs, and mists rising from thence.

It is a noted antient Archevesq,[149] the Romans first founded it and held

147   Pont-St.Esprit.
148   Le Péage-de-Roussilon?
149   Archbishopric.

it as the capital of Gallia-Celtica, and a mighty citty insomuch that upon a casuall fiering of it which occasion'd a great destruction Sæneca saies *Unaq nox interfuit inter urbem maximam et nullam.* Here are still many monuments of antiquity, and inscriptions on buriall-stones in several parts of this citty. In the garden of the Ursuline nunns are yet to bee seene Roman baths under ground, made of large firm stone, with rows of arches leading into one another. Upon an hill out of the towne are 2 arches of an aquæduct, which is said to have been 15 leagues in length for supply of this citty; all the outside stone of the wall of it was cutt in diamond, or lozange-worke. In the garden of the Minim Friers stand the ruines of a Roman cirque some say an amphitheater, but the ruines are so inconsiderable tis hard to judge what it was. There are four very bigg marble pillars of a blackish colour, which did belong to a temple dedicated to Augustus antiently, and are now in an old church which is cal'd the church of St Enoy[150] as I remember and stands allmost on the same ground.

In the church of the Carmes are 4 lofty Italian columnes of black-marble with capitols of Corinthian worke, all the bodies of entire stone, and an excellent tablet of painting over the altar donne by the excellent Salvietti. Almost opposite to this church in the midle of the streete stands the tombeau d'deus Amænds, or the tombe of the 2 lovers made of large stone and arch't over; which is suppose'd to have been a phane or place for pagan worship; yet a lying frier had the confidence to tell us that it was the tombe of Herod, and Herodias. In the Jacobines church are likewise 8 stately pillars of black marble. In St Irenees church most of the pavement is of mosaique worke, at the entrance you find 6 latine verses donne in the same. Wee mounted to the top of a high cliff where wee saw Nostre-Dame-d'Furvier, the place where Thomas of Becket retreated from the fury of Henry 2. Afterwards wee went to the house of the Grand Chartereus, who had a curious chappel and the cloyster all painted with the history of St Bruno their patron; but the principall relation is that of the dead man rising from his coffin who cri'd out thrise

> *Justo Dei judicio accusatus sum*
> *Justo Dei judicio judicatus sum*
> *Justo Dei judicio condemnatus sum.*

The grand gallery into which all their doores of their chambers enter makes a verry faire show. Their garden looks downe upon the rivers and the towne most delightfully affording a kind of ravishing prospect. In a sommer house on the left side I saw a Roman inscription on a stone in the wall.

150   Saint Irenaeus bisop of Lyons c.177-202?

Wee went downe the hill and came into the towne to the church of St John to see the phantesticall toyish clock which stands here. This clock has many necessary well-studied motions in it; but that which comes in by way of farse to the rest is this, a cock stands on the top and just upon the striking each hour claps his wings and an angel comes out of a cel brings the Virgin Mary who is there sitting in state the *Laetum Evangelisium* that she shall conceive, and bare a child, and call his name Emanuel. Then the St Esprit, or Dove descends from a litle hole and flutters about her head, and God the Father in form of an old gentleman makes the signe of the cross as well pleas'd at the salutation; then severall angels strike the chimes in manner of Haleluiah to this prælude. On the frontispiece of this church are the three leverets carv'd so cunningly that they seeme to have two yeares a piece, and yet there are but four amongst them all. Wee passt on to the La Charity wherein were upwards of 1200 persons, all kept cleanly and in good order. Wee saw their granary, and bake-house, their Botique, or Apothecaries shop, their large kitchins, their manner of dining; the apartment of the old men, and women, and that of the boyes, and girles. The place of correction for the poore female sinners. In ample manner all kept duly to their worke.

The other hospitall which is the Hostel d'Dieu is wrather bigger but not equall in cleanliness and good order; here wee saw many roomes full of sick persons of both sexes, many expos'd children, and bastards, and containes about the same number with the other; upon our going out wee bestow'd our charity upon the Box and so departed. The Jesuites college here (which I should have spoken off before more properly) is a very ample building, painted with variety of mathematicall and historicall devises, motto's, and emblemes which you may see in a particular description of it in print entitl'd La Temple de La Sagesse; they show'd us a faire library, the gallery whereof affords a pleasant prospect upon the Rhone; but tis all expresst at large in the afores'd booke so that I neede say no more. But the delightfull and principall part of the citty for recreation is Bel-Court, where most of the gallants and persons of quality resort, for the conveniency of the Mal, and cooleness of walkes.

The Mason d'Ville is a haughty, spatious building with a stately fountaine standing before it; it ha's been a litle injur'd by fire but stopt before it could doe any great mischief. At the entrade on the steps were erected 2 noble marble columes vain'd with white and red, and guarded at bottome with spikes of iron. In the Sale, or Great Hall on the left side were 2 antique tables of copper fixt in the wall; which had been found under ground, ingrav'd in latine with the commendations of Claudian the Emperour. In the first court an epigramme of Scaligers in praise of the citty of Lyons decipher'd in letters of gold; many flattering elogies on their King Luis the 14th one whereof going up staiers on the right hand spoke of the great advantages of peace the pyrinean treaty brought to Europe; saies *et Anglis Regem restituit*. Here wee saw the commedies of Venus, and Adonis, and Amphitrio stollen out of Plautus meanely acted in the Governors Hall. Wee obtain'd the favour of seeing both Monseur Serviers cabinets, the upper, and the lower, wherein was the sympatheticall watch, the water dyall, and abundance of strange motions, with many pretty knacks.

On the 2nd of 8br [October] early in the morning I departed from Lyons, giving 12 pistoles for a place for mee and my Man, and 6 sous a pound for my horde as they term it, or luggage; being allow'd tenne pound apiece free and no more, wee went by boate the first day and din'd aboard having had but poore accommodation; this night wee lodg'd at Mascon[151] lying upon the River Saone in Burgoigne. The third wee went by water to Challone[152] in Challenois in Burgoigne; it is a large towne upon the same river. Here wee took coach and 6 horses and went that night to a small bourgh in that cuntry. The 4th through a rough and wooddy cuntry to Salieu. The 5th day through an uneven barren cuntry to Vernantone[153] to lodge. The 6th wee din'd at Auxerre in Auxerrois the capitol of the province, and in the neerest part of Burgoigne to Paris. The 7th through a plentifull cuntry of vines and wallnuts, and lodg'd that night at Villeneuf L'Roy,[154] where wee mett with excellent wine both white, and read. This towne lies upon the River Yonne in Sennonois which is part of the province of Champaigne. The 8th wee travel'd through Sens the Archevesque[155] of this province and lying on the same river, and through a plentifull cuntry of corne, leaving the mighty chatteau of Fountaine Bleau (which is directly upon the borders of the Isle of France) upon the left hand environ'd with rocks, and woods; wee came to lodge at Melun in the Isle. The last day having but eleven leagues, wee passt by many beautifull seates by the River Seyne and before 12 of the clock arriv'd at Paris. Here I remain'd about a fortnight and equip't my self and then took Messenger and came to Calais and by the 8th of 9br [October] our stile arriv'd at London.

Hoc amo quod possum qualibet ire via.

151   Macon.
152   Chalon-sur-Saone.
153   Vermenton.
154   Villeneuve-sur-Yonne.
155   Archbishopric.

7
A TOUR ROUND WALES

A journy beganne August 9th 1676
and continued throughout the principality of Wales

O N THE DAY aforesaid wee left London, and lodge'd the first night at Beckensfield, and on the 10th to Oxford, where having view'd the Colleges, and observ'd many superstitious Roman ceremonies to bee yet retained in their chappels, to the shame of such as pretend to bee Reformers, wee came at last to see the Theater so much talk't off for the renowne of Shelden the Archbishop and founder; this is plaine and low, with a cupolo too small for the building, and seems something like a pidgeon-house to the schooles that stand by it. The antiquities which are the Marmora Arundelianæ, and are now marked with H. and S. signifying their late founders, are plac't in ill-favord neeches in a wall encompassing this Theater too meane for the nobleness of

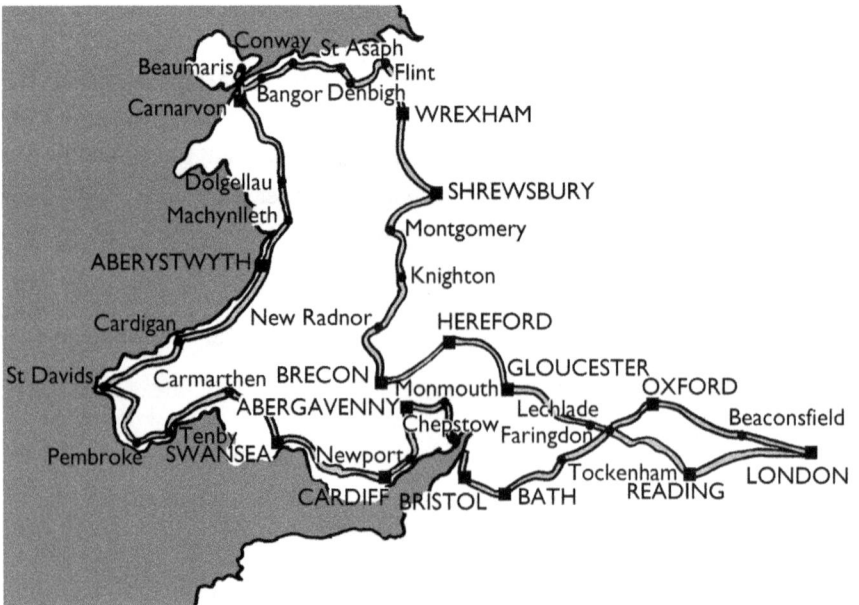

such rarities. On the 11th wee lodg'd at Farindon[156] on the 12th and 13th at Tockenham: the 14th at Bath. The 15th and 16th at Bristoll, so flourishing for the trading part of a citty, but short for any beauty, or state in building Redcliff Church being the prime thing show'd to strangers.

Chepstow. Monmouthshire

ON THE 17TH wee beganne to enter upon our progresse, wee ferried our horses over from Ast[157] to Beechly,[158] and so came to this towne belonging to the Marquess of Worcester, where was kept a small garrison of a Foot Company as a kind of a check upon the Welchmen. Comming in wee rode over a high woodden bridge to passe the Wye, the tide flowing to a greate heigth. Within it wee saw an old castle built along upon a rock but demolisht, and a church allmost in the same condition. This is the entrance into Monmouthshire which by the stat[ute] of the 27th of Henry 8 c.27th came to bee annext to England, and reckon'd in the English Circuits.[159]

On the 18th wee came to Monmouth the shire-towne; where Wye and Munnow[160] meeting together make one channel; comming hither wee passt by an old seate cal'd Troy belonging to the Marquess of Worcester. Here wee saw a small fragment of an aged castle wherein the puissant Henry 5 was borne; an old church with the ruines of a priory adjoin'd to it; and a generous foundation of a well indow'd almshouse, the way hither rocky, and the descent into the towne bad. They show'd likewise the remaines of some carv'd work in wood which they say was his cradle.

On the 19th wee went for Abergavenny through an inclos'd cuntry, yet much better way than wee had before. Here wee mett with good accommodation; the towne is inviron'd with a broken wall, the streets well pav'd, the edifices pretty decent; here is held the greatest market for Flannings throughout Wales. Hard by stand the ruines of a castle belonging to the barons of Abergavenny so renown'd of old. In a chapel on the right side of the chief church are to be seene many old monuments belonging to this family: amongst which one lies with a hogg slaine at his feete, which they explaine to you by this strange story. That this Lord comming suddenly into the Castle found the

156 Faringdon.

157 Aust.

158 Beachley.

159 The country was divided into six circuits for the Assize Courts which judges from the London courts held in the county towns twice a year. They dealt with many serious crimes.

160 River Monnow.

cradle wherein his child lay overturn'd, and the flore smear'd with blood, and his gray-hound lying by all bloody; hee not doubting but his child was slaine by this dogg rashly drew his sword and slew <kil'd> the poore creature; presently after lifting up the cradle found the babe alive, and in a corner of the roome a serpent worried to death, which too late convinc't him of his error, whereupon to expiate the offence he slew himself and so compleated the dismall tragedy. Another was the tombe of a young lady of this family, who walking under the castle wall with a squirrel in her arms, suffer'd it to escape from her; she earnest to pursue, not regarding the precipe of the banke, fell headlong into the trench and so ended her life. The Roman Catholiques swarme much here the present young Baron being of the same principle. On the 20th wee went through close lanes till wee came to Carleon, formerly knowne by the names of Venta Silurum, and Isca, the seate of the fam'd Brittish Arthur; in a meadow litle without the towne, they show'd us a wide hollow space, where his Round Table stood at which hee entertain'd his tilting knights; the towne lies rambling along upon the River Uske.

Glamorganshire. Caerdiff

ON THE 21 wee passt through Newport and so enter'd the cuntry, and came to Tredhegar the mansion house of Mr Morgan who had allmost compleated a faire structure of brick with stables and wall'd-courts answerable, esteemed one of the best piles in all the cuntry. Hence wee bent our course to Cardiff the capitall of the shire seated on the River Tave. Here wee saw the old castle belonging to the Earle of Pembrook, formerly built by Fitz-Hamon the Norman for a reception of him and his twelve knights whose arms are hung up in an escucheon in the hall; hee allso fortified the towne of which there are but meane remainders. In the castle wee were show'd into dungeon where the unfortunate Robert Courthois was detain'd prisoner for the space of 26 yeares by his unmercifull brother Henry the first. See what ambitious man will doe to obtaine a Crowne.

Landaff

TWO MILES DISTANT from hence stands the litle and inconsiderable city of Landaff scarse deserving the name of a village containing not above tenn or a dossen houses in all. Wee were induc'd to walke hither in order to view a sorry decayed cathedrall, in which were some antient tombs. And on the back of the episcopall chair the Virgin Mary painted mounting to heaven by the helpe of four angels; at her feete one Marshall a former bishop of the See was kneeling with this sentence comming out of his mouth.

O: virgo scandens, sis Marshallo cælica pandens.

Whether it has been disregarded by the protestant bishops since the Reformation, or remains as a relict of antiquity I leave to the reader to judge. Hard by are the ruines of a poore litle castle. On the 22nd being a hazy day wee declin'd going to St Donnets,[161] and went through Cowbridge; and lodg'd at a poore place cal'd Bridgend.

Swansey

O N   T H E   2 3 D wee came to Margham[162] the prime seate of Sir Edward Mansel; having 2 large parks adjoining to it both well-woodded, and stor'd with deere. The house is somewhat old and irregular, affording litle to the view but a large stable, and a pleasant bowling-greene; here wee were hospitably received and this night came to Swansey the chief port of the shire; the towne is somewhat large but very ordinary for accommodation; having litle other trade than the venting of pit coles to France, and some other parts. Here are the ruines of an old castle now converted to a glass-house.

Caermardenshire

O N   T H E   2 4 T H leaving the sea-side wee made up into the cuntry over the mountains and came to Caermarthen lying upon the River Toye or Tovye[163] which receives the advantage of the tide though so farr in the cuntry. At this place Mirlin the Brittish Wizard had his birth. The towne is pretty well-built of stone and of an indifferent bigness; injoying a small trade by some barques that pass up and downe. Wee chanced to bee here at the Assizes, and saw the 2 Judges in scarlet walking to the Towne Hall, with a trumpet and a small traine of attendance; a kind of a Welch representation of state. Nothing more but a large ill-favord church, and a ruin'd castle converted to a prison. Historians tell us that this towne was named by the Romans Maridunum, and all the inhabitants of the South Division of Wales cal'd the Silures.

Pembrokshire

O N   T H E   2 5 T H wee made downe to the sea-side againe, and came to the port of Tinby[164]; where wee found many colepits lying neere the towne,

161   Welsh St Donats.
162   Margam.
163   River Towy.
164   Tenby.

which is the only trade it depends upon. It was fortified with a strong wall, and a castle built on a rock adjoinining to the towne reaching farr into the sea: but overthrowne, and demolisht in the late times by the victorious parlament forces. Since which it has had so litle incouragement, and is so thinly inhabited, that the streets are become desolate, and the houses generally runne to ruine. The maine support it now hath is a small peere made of loose stone, which by reason of its scarcity induces some vessels to come and anchor here.

Pembrooke

ON THE 26TH wee came hither, where from the name of the shire one might have expected a better towne; but instead of that wee found it wrather worse than the former; it is a peninsula the tide flowing allmost round it. In a rock by the water-side wee were show'd a wide cave; which wee enter'd and found that by meanes of a high arch the eccho did reverberate strongly; the people call it the Ougan which in the Welch tongue signifies a cave or hole. In the castle here the extorting Henry 7th was borne, which has been capacious and large; but since laide in ruine by the daring Oliver Cromwell.

Haverford-West

AFTER DINNER WEE tooke horse and went over at Burton Ferry a creeke belonging to the noble and magnificent Mylford-Haven; a place that for its naturall commodiousness for ships, surpasses all the ports in Europe besides having not the least help of art. Hence wee went to lodge at Haverford-West: built on the side of a hill; with a remnant of an old castle. Wee came hither at the time the Assizes were held for the County.

On the 27th wee went off from hence, and so farr found the south-parts plentifull both with corn and grasse but here beganne the alteration. We set forward for St Davids seated on the farthest nooke of the southwest part of Wales, in a wilde and barren cuntry voide of all sort of accommodation, the place itself wrather like the skeleton, or carcass of some meane towne, then the resemblance of citty; being nothing but a ruine of miserable thacht cottages showing poverty beyond comparison. The churchmen most unmercifully devoure all the proffits of the place and leave the poore to shift for themselves, being seldom resident but just at the Audit dayes to receive their revenew; they uphold a thinne outward shadow of devotion, and a small organ like a bagpipe with half-dozen grating-singing at 16£ a yeare apiece to carry on the grandeur of cathedral servise as they call it. This Bell and the Dragon crew share about 4000£ a yeare amongst 'um, and yet leave the church in so despicable a condition, that it lies like those at London after the Fire; above half of it allready dropt to the ground, and the rest fairly following. The Reverend old Bishop he's received 6000£ fines besides the standing income of the See, yet never preacht here, or ever saw the place but once since the Restauration, a good signe of laboring in the Gospell. Hee suffers his pallace to drop to the ground which might easily have been kept up for a 100£ laide out at his first comming to it. It is sd Henry 8 spar'd this church, at the Grand Dissolution of the Abbeys, because the Earle of Richmond father to Henry 7 was interred here; whose marble monument stands in the midle of the quire; on each hand lie 2 stone figures carv'd in antient armour, which they say are teuthors[165] former princes of the cuntry; but of what part unknowne; onely report saies one of them fell in batle for his luxury in depraving and seducing another princes wife. Neere to this lies the tombe of Anselme bishop of this place, whose epitaph ought to bee inserted as a testimony of the learning of that age. Round his head in a phylactery is this verse

petra dic sic, quod Anselmus Episcopus est hic.

Amongst the rubbish wee discover'd the tombe of a phisitian with this inscription.

Hic jacet Medicus cujus Ruina, monstrat quod Morti, non obsistit Medicina.

which shows that the authour of it had somthing a superior genius, than hee that made that on the great prelate. They annually choose a maior for this despicable place cal'd a citty, and the chief see of all Wales.

Cardiganshire

ON THE 28TH wee travelled a long way through a poore cuntry and came to Cardigan (the head towne of the shire) seated on the Rover Tivy,[166] and lying commodious for trade as many of the Welch townes doe, had they but a stock, and good laws for incouragement. The tide makes eight foot water at the towne, and flows four mile beyond it. As the case now stands it is but meane, and small, yet here wee had pretty good entertainment. A large bridge over this river, and some remnant of a castle whose foundation has been worne away with the tide. Here wee reposed one whole day, and then departed.

165   This appears to be a stab at the Welsh word for princes, *tywysog*.
166   River Teifi.

Aberustith[167]

O N THE 30TH wee went off from hence the way proving difficult, and unusuall wee were constrained to take a Guide on horseback; wee wrode over a desperate præcipice on the sea-side; the cuntry wild, open, and stony, yet indifferent plenty of corne; but desolation and scarsity of people. Wee lodg'd this night at a miserable village lying on the side of the Westerne Sea cal'd Aberistuyth, where were the ruines of a litle castle on a rock; great store of herrings and other fish along the coast, but the trade slighted for want of stock; by which meanes the accommodation is very poore.

Machenlet[168]

O N THE 31 wee sett forward againe to pass through the remainder of this cuntry which was extreme hilly, and desert, yet corne enough to show the industry of the Improvers; about midday we came, and took a wholmy repast in a mechanick village cal'd Machenlet.

Merionethshire

H AVING BEEN INFORM'D that our way was now too difficult, wee determine'd to take a Guide and so went forwards for Dolgelthe[169] in Merionethshire, having gonne by the great Plinilimon Hill a litle below Machenlet. This part of the cuntry, and all the inhabitants were antiently term'd the Ordovices. Our way now prov'd wooddy and melancholly, winding strangly betweene the rocks, and for 3 Miles before wee came to the towne wonderfully craggy, and full of great loose stones, vast lakes, and mighty falls of water, which made a hideous noise pen'd in betweene the rocks. The towne lies in a bottom and is meane enough in any conscience as to entertainment or any thing else thats good yet reckon'd as the wonder of Northwales for three things. First its walls which are two miles in height, next an unusuall entring into a towne, which is riding under water for your passage, and then a growing <seeming> steeple in which the bell hangs. All which comicall wonders are thus easily explain'd. The walls are the rocks that seeme to inviron and hang over the towne. The going under water is the spout of an overshott mill which is sett athwart the way, so that you cannot avoide passing under it if you will goe into the towne. And as for the growing steple tis nothing but a yew-tree in which they hang up a litle bell to summon people to church for want of a better conveniency.

167   Aberystwyth.
168   Machynlleth.
169   Dolgellau.

Carnarvanshire

ON THE FIRST of 7br [September] taking a fresh Guide from hence wee bent our course through the rest of Merionethshire, along a rough and allmost inaccessible way, finding no accommodation for above 30 long miles. After a whole dayes tedious, and incessant riding) our Guide (through lakes and desolate places brought us much within night to the towne of Carnarvan the chief of the shire; where wee found some refreshment after a long labour. This towne is pretty compact and lies on the sea-side opposite to Anglesey; 'tis inviron'd with a high wall and was once noted for a lofty and stately castle, the seate of the warlike Edward 1 wherein his degenerat sonne and successor to the Crowne Edward 2 was borne, in a tower cal'd Eagle Tower, there being some carv'd Eagles on the batlements to this day. The cunstable of the castle is continually Maior of the towne; the ruines of it was in the family of Bodviles, and by mariage came to the eldest sonne of the Lord Roberts.

Anglesey

ON THE 2ND of 7br [September] wee went forward to Porthætey[170] ferry, and so enter'd our horses in a boate and went over into the Isle of Anglesey, which wee found very rocky; and notwithstanding the inhabitants boast so much of their plenty of corne, yet in many parts it seem'd barren enough. By night wee came to lodge at a towne cal'd Beaumaris founded by Edward 1 who gave it this French name from its flatt, or cleare scituation on marshy ground. This place is very poore depending generally on the resort of people that goe over for Ireland. Here lies a ?l.. ruin'd castle towards the shore, and on the other side of the towne the seate of the Lord Buckly.

Bangor

ON THE 3RD of 7br [September] wee retourn'd from the Island, and ferried over a broad part of Menai River and came into Carnarvanshire againe, and so proceeded to the episcopall citty of Bangor being Sunday, whereby wee had the opportunity of hearing cathedrall servise and a sermon celebrated in the Welch tongue. It is but a meane church; great part of it together with the citty (which they say was then two miles long though now but small) was burnt by that sturdy rebell Owen Glendore whose tombe wee here saw. It seems the clergy of the age (in regard to their Soveraigne) caus'd him to bee inter'd in the outward part of the wall of the church, half in and half out, to remaine (as they suppos'd) a marke of infamy to posterity. After dinner wee left this place.

170   There was a ferry at Porthaethwy until a bridge was built in the 1820s. https://
www.heneb.co.uk/cadwprojs/cadwreview2006/menaistraits06.html

Aberconway

O UR WAY TO come hither lay over the greate precipice on the side of Pen-menmaure which wee achiev'd, and by night came to this towne which lies upon the River Conway and the farthest part northward of Carnarvanshire. It is fenc't about with an old stone-wall with watch-towers, and lies commodious for navigation by the benefit of tides that flow before the towne. Wee were show'd the remaines of a stately castle built upon a rock on the water side (belonging to the Lord Conway) wherein was a well of mighty depth and circumference, with the ruines of the princes great Hall as they cal'd it. Taking boate from hence wee mett with some quicc sands.

St Asaph

O N THE 4TH Instant having passt the river wee went onward to the cathedral citty of St Asaph in Flintshire which is so sadly meane that it could scarse afford us any accommodation, and worse than any of them but St Davids. A poore, rude, melancholly church only the quire something tolerable with the Bishops Seate, and the old carv'd stoules for the prebends and singing-men. The pallace is but plain and ordinary but it seems the see is wealthy enough bringing in 15, or 1600£ pr ann., which tends to no other good than to mumble a few Welch, and make a lamentable noise amongst themselves; for they have scarse any other auditory, there being so few inhabitants amongst them. After a pitifull repast wee tended from hence to

Denbigh

W EE NOW WENT through the pleasant litle vale of Cluyd which the Welch call Duffren Cluyd, and by night took up our lodgin in this towne the head of Denbighshire. Tis a long, narrow towne but as twere of one good streete. On the top of a high hill stands a large demolisht castle which had been a garrison in the late times but destroyed since the Restauration. The River Cluyd runs by it. In it wee found good entertainment.

Holy-well

T HE NEXT MORNING being on the 5th Instant wee enter'd Flintshire againe and went to the votary towne of Holy-well, which is but small only depending upon the resort of pilgrims, and superstitious zealots. Wee first came to a decayed chappel dedicated to faire St Winifred, upon a small rising rock, where they say the virgin was forc't, and afterwards had her head struck off by a goatish Welch-prince. Her head rowling downe afterwards pitch't in the place where this spring rises up, which indeede is a delicate water, and has a strong ebullition; its cover'd over with an arch of stone of good worke; a relique of rejected popery but now much desired againe, as is manifest by the many people that come thither. On the entrance on the right side was a small crucifix carv'd in stone, on the left was this prayer *O Sancte Winifrede virgo, et Martyr ora pro nobis.* The pebles of the fountain are speckle'd red as the effects of the Saints blood; and the moss growing in the current from it has a sweete sent like muske, and retaines it for a long time as wee found by experiment. The votaries make their procession round the spring so many times as injoyn'd by the priest, mumbling of prayers, and entring the water ever and anon; some come for remission of sinns, others to be eas'd of aches, and paines, and distempers just as the spirit moves them.

Flint

THIS EVENING WEE arriv'd at this towne the chief of the shire where wee were well accommodated. This place likewise is well scituate for trade the sea flowing up into the channel of the River Dee. Here wee were show'd the fragments of a castle wherein that misguided King Richard the 2nd was seized, and detain'd afterwards in prison in the tower by Henry of Bullingbrook to whome he surrendred the Crowne in full parlament. The cuntry in all these northward parts fertil enough.

Wrexham

ON THE 6 of this Instant wee travelled on by the English side of Wales opposite to Cheshire, and came to lodge at this towne which is in Denbighshire and is wrather larger than any of the Welch townes having a small streame running by it. The chief thing of note is a large church with a well-carv'd lofty tower. They told us here one pretty fansy of the inhabitants, that at the Kings Restauration the frantick rable being transported with joy made a bonfire on top of the tower which melted the leads thereof, and had not providence diverted it had cetainly burnt downe this faire structure and indangerd the whole towne besides.

Montgomery

ON THE 7TH parting from hence wee made a stepp to Shrewsbury, and the next day being the 8th wee retourned into Wales againe, and passing through Cherbury came to lodge at this poore Shire-towne of Montgomery consisting of a few meane paper-built houses; and notwithstanding the lowness of their conditions they told us they were forc't to make a purse of 20£ each

Assizes for satisfying their hungry judges, who have sufficient salaries pd 'um
by the king besides. In the church wee saw some monuments of the family of
the Lord Herberts; and an old demolisht castle standing aloft upon a rock in
the parke the seate of the family till ruin'd in the late times, by order of the
Goverment least it should bee possest by their enemies the Cavaliers. In this
place the Lord wrote his fam'd Treatise de Veritate.

New-Radnor

ON THE 9TH wee went onward and repasted at Knighton and came
to lodg at this place, being a more miserable shire towne than any of
the rest, scarsly affording beds, or ought of entertainment; and reduc't to the
degree of poverty that they are forc'd to let fall their Market. Here wee enter'd
the Silures cuntry again (as they term'd it of old) wee mett with nothing here
but some few stones, or rubbish of a castle. Old Radnor is quite worne out,
and Prestayne is now accompted the most considerable towne.

Brecknock

ON THE 10TH being Sunday wee travel'd all day finding few people,
and no place for reception, by the evening wee came to Breknok the
shire towne, which I conceive to bee the best of Wales for the conveniency of
travellers. Wee saw the great church and the priory, and allso the College to
which are appertaining 22 prebends all in the donation, and disposall of the
Bishop of St Davids. The ruine of a castle belonging to Mr Morgan of Tredegar.
It is well water'd with the River Uske; round about it a mountanous cuntry.

Hereford

ON THE 11TH through a barre, and hilly Cuntry wee came to the towne
of Hereford lying upon the River Wye. It is somwhat large; for its loyalty
in keeping out the Scots the late king confer'd a coate of arms upon them with
this motto *Invicta fidelitatis præmium*, and for this cause the present king spar'd
their walls, when he order'd those of Gloucester, and Coventry to bee throwne
downe. This episcopall see has an antient cathedrall with a lofty spire ledded.
The names of many of their old Bishops are painted afresh in neeches on the
right isle of the church by the quire for the information of strangers, by the
care of Deane Hodges.

Gloucester

ON THE 13TH Instant wee arriv'd at this citty which is large and seated
in a faire plaine of meadows on the bankes of Severn. This citty is the

less regarded for its former delinquency, and obstinate holding out for the parlament against a mighty army of the kings, which was bash'd before it by the industrious endeavours of their Governour Massey. It is supposed that for this cause their walls were demolisht soone after the Restauration for all the Act of Indemnity. Here is a stately cathedrall, in which is the noted whispering place and the tombs of three very famour persons viz Edward 2, Robert Duke of Normandy eldest sonne to the Conqueror, and Humphry d' Bohun Duke of Hereford as I take it.

On the 14th wee made for Leachlade that night, meeting with nothing remarkable but the windows of the parish church of Fayrford (a small village in the way) wheron was curiously painted the history of the Bible in generall; only a little injur'd by time. The most observable was the window of the Supreme Judgment, on which was a feate fansie of the painters, who had drawne a blew devil with horns driving a naked woman to hell in a yellow wheelebarrow, for scolding at her husband as the clarke told us, but we suppose'd it cuckholding.

On the 15th wee went for Reading. On the 16th to Windesore where wee saw his Majesties new-buildings and the intended fortifications, and the mock-Mestricht. As allso St Georges chappel in which are many reliques of popery. The next day being Saturday wee ferried the River for Colebrook, and so directly for London.

8

A SMALL VOYAGE TO THE CHANNEL ISLANDS

A small Voyage beganne on the 20th of Apr: 1677
Cherbour[171]

[Note: for map see page 74]

O N THE 25TH of April this year wee sett out from Lymington in Hampshire in a small High about 15 tunne and pass'd the Needles, and made out to sea, and sail'd all that night, and by eight of the clock next morning came in view of Orney, or Alderney; but the wind slacking wee could not make this island, and were forc'd to fall away with the tide, along by the coast of Normandy for severall leagues. At length by 9 a clock of the night wee anchor'd before Cherbour, and went ashore in our boate and lodg'd in the Fauxbourge. The Governour was the Marquess d' Fontney. The towne lies open to the sea is poore and has but litle trade, only now and then wooll and some few commodities that they steale ashore in the night. It is immur'd with a high old wall and a chateau within that inhabited by the Governour. Antiently it was in the hands of the English, in remarque whereof wee were show'd an old port now stopt up out of which they march't upon quitting of it; over it some broken remainders of the Arms of England. One onely church here built by the English, and noe Religious House, except a poore Hermitage a mile from the towne at the foot of a rock and another on top thereof. Wee staide here all the Sunday and for diversion saw the youth shoot in their fusees (for the prize) at the target; the victor conducted home in triumph, with drumms beating and musick playing before him. On the 22nd being Sunday about 8 in the evening wee went aboard againe, and about twelve of the clock that night weigh'd anchor, and sail'd by the Normandy coast, and about day passt the Raze, wee afterwards made up by Alderney, and came in sight of Sarke (both appertaining to Sir George

171   Cherbourg.

Cartwright) then by Arke and Arm, all a dangerous rocky coast; and by 10 of the clock that morning made into the peere of Garnsee.[172]

Garnsee. St Peters towne.

THE PEERE FOR the incouragement of trading was first beganne by Queene Elizabeth and is at this time an advantageous harbour for ships in passing betweene the hither parts of France and England; it is wall'd on each side, and pav'd a top, which affords the townes-people a convenient walke, and prospect to the sea, and likewise a considerable benefit in trade. The towne lies upon the side of a hill on the sea shore reaching about a mile in length. The prime magistrate is the provo[st] that mannages the towne affairs. Here wee mett with great plenty of Bourdeaux wine at 5 sou's a quart, and cider, and beare very cheape but bread, and meate very deare, there being generally a scarsity of corn in the island, and this yeare a great derth of cattle hapning by the extreme severity of the winter. The principall manufacture of the place is knitting insomuch that in every corner you see nothing but schooles of young women a knitting. Each Saturday is the Market, and over night they kill their beasts on the shore, and in the morning hang them upon the sides of the houses in every streete to invite the purchasers as they are passing along, and not to give you the trouble to come to a Market-House.

About a quarter of a mile from this towne on a little island, or rock that stands incompass'd with the sea is Cornet-Castle which is the strength and guard of the island, and the place of residence for the Governour. Hither wee came in a boate where wee beheld a spectacle of great ruine, and destruction; which is related to bee thus. About four yeares since in the month of 10br [October] the Governour my Lord Hatton and his family being present, there hapned a violent storme of thunder, and lightning; and a magazine of 200 barrels of powder which lay in a vault in a round-tower about the middle of the castle blew up and destroyed allmost the whole structure; so that to this time it remaines only a heape of rubbish. Many persons were destroy'd by this misfortune, whereof the governours mother, and his Lady were of the number. He himself miraculously preserv'd having been blowne out of his bed upon a rock only a litle bruis'd. At the entrance is a small space for a guard, and a few iron gunns mounted wrather for show, than defence. The king is at the charge of three or four companyes for this place, and the standing Militia consists of 2000 – of the inhabitants; yet their maine security depends on the rocks that stand thick on the shore and seeme to impale the island. Here and there upon the open and naked parts are some old iron gunns planted on the shore, of

172   Guernsey.

litle validity against an enemy. The land is fertil enough with grass, and well inclosed with stone walls which inviron about an acre or two at a time; corne is not very plentifull here except what is brought in by shipping, their bread for the most part gristy. Their upper grounds towards the sea-side poore, and rocky.

Having obtain'd horses wee travel'd about to see the chatteau in the vale of St Michael, a meane inconsiderable ruine, the church of St Sampson, the Abby in the vale. Nostre Dame de Castel; these salt-panns, and the greate pond belonging to the king. The goverment is according to the old laws of Normandy, every parish has his representative, who by the name of 12 Jurats and as Justices of Peace, mannage the whole affairs of the nation with the assistance of a Bailie and 2 Shireeves. If at any time the Governour interpose to medle with any thing they recken it not d' jure but in compliance, and condescension to his Majesty. Every parish church has 2 fieldpieces, and an amunition waggon immediately ready for furnishing the Militia if neede bee.

The king is the great impropriator and and (sic) receives the 10ths out of most lands, and has a fine upon every saile or alienacion and the nomination of all their ministers or clergy; the superintendent whereof is a Deane as the Bishop is with us. Hee has power to excommunicate, and silence the ministers as he pleases; yet reckon'd under the jurisdiction of the Bishop of Winchester. All the sæcular magistrates are made by vote or popular election. The king has likewise certaine old rents, or fee-farms from their lands; so that in the whole it amounts to 800 or 1000£ pr ann. which is left to the management, and advantage of the Governour. The livings of the ministers are commonly reckon'd at 60£ pr ann. one with another. The French tongue is generally spoken in the villages by the peasants. Their principall houses are all stone with tourels running up after the Norman manner and only an arch of a gate with a litle grove of ashes both on the front, and reare of the house which seems pretty. Men of families and estates are the Beauvoies, Caries, Merchants and such like. The best estates here seldome rises higher than 5 or 600 pounds a yeare, because the descents are of a strang nature, vizi a gavelkind rarely to bee mett withall, both sonnnes, and daughters sharing an equall, and identicall proportion. They lie more southward than wee, which occasions a forwarder Spring; yet their Winter is more harsh and severe than ours. Most of their utensils are brough[t] from Normandy even to their ploughs that they use in tillage. They pay neither excise, custome, chimney-money, or taxes of any sort whatever unless it bee parochiall rates. They seeme most inclinable, and propense in nature to their old cuntrymen of France and no doubt were it not for these privileges, and immunities would lay-hold on the next opportunity of joining with them.

Wee remained wind-bound here to Sunday the 29 of April and then about 9 of the clock in the morning wee made out of the peere and sett saile for Jarsey. Wee first made the Corbiere a great rock lying out in the sea upon the west-point of the island, then wee made into the port of St Obien, or St Albans about 5 of the clock, upon a rock under a small fort commanded by an indigent officer one Serjeant King. Having supped at this litle village in the evening wee march't over the sands by the sea-side and about night came to the towne of St Hillary.

Jarsey. St Hillary's towne

DIRECTLY UPON THE opening into a plentifull valley lies the towne and without doubt was formerly the chief harbour of the island, till by process of time it came to bee choak'd up by the sands. It seems as it were one open streete with a large Market-place and by it an old church with a flatt low tower, wherein wee met with one only tombe sett up for Captain Norry's in commicall Latine verse. Nigh the towne wee ascended a rock to take a farther prospect into the valley: from whose top the late parlament souldiers found a way to fire granadoe shells of 500 weight into Eliz: Castle being above a mile distant in the sea which caus'd 'um to surrender whereof more hereafter.

The Morrow after wee came hither about the time of ebbing water in the beginning of the afternoon wee passt over a beech (much like that at Hurst Castle but not so thick with pebles) and came to the rock on which this castle is founded. It was beganne by Sir Walter Raleigh (in the raigne of Queene Eliz: out of the ruines of a religious house dedicated to St Hillary) who gave it her name; and by some it is called New-Castle; being the latest founded there of any on the summit of a rock a litle distance from the castle, and flow'd about by the sea at high water; there is yet to bee seene St Hillary's chamber hew'd out of the rock, with a small place for his bed (as is vainly imagin'd) cover'd over head; and some few loop-holes of prospect on the sea. The ascent is dangerous; neere the foott of it is a great chimney in the walls, cal'd St Hilary's kitchen. Wee found an ample space of ground within the castle walls; the bastions firm and nigh a hundred iron gunns mounted and in good order. Going up the steps by the iron-gate wee saw carv'd in stone the arms of Queene Elizabeth and of one of the Paulets Governour of the place in her raigne. At the upper part of it on a large pav'd battery, are the lodgings in which Charles the 2nd lay upon his first expulsion from England where the Scotch-Commissioners treated with him; they are vaulted, and above are many tanks, and cisterns of leade for receiving of rainwater for a supply. About the midle of the castle wee look't on the ruines of a chappel which had been blowne up by the granadoe-shells fir'd from a rock by the towne as wee mention'd before, which likewise broke into a magazine under this chappel, and destroyed many persons frequenting divine service. Wee were courteously received by Captaine Rawleigh who gave us the Freedome of the Castle, and admitted us to discourse with Colonel Temple one of the Regicides who for many yeares had been kept prisoner here. The next day being the first of May intending to see the island wee gott horses, and went through the parishes of St Saviours and Greville; where wee saw a litle old church with 2 field-peeces in it after the custome of Garnzee.

The land is extreame pleasant, and delightfull to the view; with neat enclosures of pasture, and corne, and large orchards of fruit-trees. The lanes in which wee travel guarded with high-bankes, and on each side sett with rows of elms, or oakes, which grow lofty and meete at the top; whereby you may ride as secure from the weather as if in an arbour. Wee wrode in this manner till wee came to Mount Orgueil (or the old castle) scituate on the east side of the island upon a high-mounting rock so cal'd from it's pride or loftiness; tis saide it was first founded by Julius Cæsar from whome the island is nominated Cesarea. Here wee beheld much of antiquity of building; but irregular and confused; the batteries not in so good order, nor so well gunn'd as the other: yet the place seemes to bee well enough guarded by the sea, and adjacent rocks, which threaten terror enough against any invaders. Wee were here caresst by the Lieutenant Governour Sir Herbert Luxsford a true old hum-drum Cavalier, fitt for nothing but to bee laide by, or throwne in a corner, like old shooes. While wee were here wee saw 2 regiments of the island Militia draw up and make their approches to the castle and fire (being Muster day) and were afterward saluted by the great-gunns from the castle. Wee retourned home againe that night the lower way through St Clements parish and came to the towne againe.

The next morning wee walk'd over the sands and retourned to our litle vessel at St Albans againe, where wee imbarg'd for Garnsee and came into the peere about 2 of the clock in the morning. It is observable that this island breedes no venemous creatures whereas Jarsey abounds with toades and such like from whence if any chance to bee brought over to the isle they dye immediately upon comming a-shore. Wee rested here all the day, and about 4 of the clock next morning made away (as before) betweene the rocky islands, and then alongst the Raze by Normandy, and so steer'd northwest for England. Wee remain'd this whole day upon the ocean meeting with nothing but a tierse of claret which was hoist aboard; the remainder of some miserable wreck. All this night wee continued at sea, and the next day about 8 in the evening wee came safe on land at the key at Limington.

9
A JOURNEY TO DERBYSHIRE

**A Journey beganne about the 20th
of August 1677**

H AVING RESTED AT Thingdon[173] in Northamptonshire, about the space of
five dayes after wee had come from London wee took our journey from
hence in the morning, and the same day baited at Harborough, and so to the
towne of Leicester, from thence directly to Loughburrough in Leicestershire
where wee lodg'd that night. The day following wee went to Darby to dinner;
and so to Crich (vulgarly cal'd Crites) a solitary village plac'd in the rocks of the
Peake cuntry. The observables of this towne were but few, only in the parish
church an antique tombe belonging to the family of the Ferriers or Ferris's, in
the conclusion of whose epitaph were these words *Anno a Virginis partu 1588*,
which kind of date I have not usually mett withall. Hence wee took a Guide
(by reason of the uncouthness of the cuntry) and travelling along wee passt by
an old seate belonging to the family of the Babingtons cal'd (in a barren heathy
cuntry) cal'd Dethick, forfeited to the Crowne in the raigne of Queene Elizabeth
for treason. Afterwards wee came through the rocky parke of Chatsworth, and
went downe into Eddin a poore village adjoining to this place, where wee sett
up our horses, and sent to know whether wee might bee permitted to see the
castle of Chatsworth (the seate of the present Earle of Devonshire) which being
granted wee forthwith repaired thither, where wee found a lofty quadrangular
building of freestone rais'd by Eliz Countess of Shrewsbury primo Mariæ [1st
year of Mary's reign] as is manifest from an inscription on the front thereof;
which seems to bee regular, but some other parts of this building towards the
upper end doe nowayes correspond. The apartment towards the garden was
at this time reforming, and altering according to the new mode. Going up

---

173   Findon, alternatively known as Thingdon (Lewis's *Topographical Dictionary*).
Walker possibly had property here. There was a Walker charity for a boy's free
school recorded in *the National Gazetteer of Great Britain and Ireland* (1868).

the stair-case which had been newly inlarg'd (to a great cost) yet the heigth, no way answering the breadth, wee came at last to the Chambers of State, or best roomes. Amongst these was the chamber of Mary Queene of Scots the infamous mother of King James who was here kept prisoner by Queene Elizabeth then the chamber of the Earle of Leicester. A gallery of costly inlaide worke in prospective, with a chamber of the same adjoining to it. Most of the chimny-peeces of antique worke in alabaster dugg in those parts. A kind of a hanging garden cutt out in walkes under the rocks with basins, jetto's and fountains but as yet unfinisht. The ponds before the house are supplyde by the River Derwent which streames along by it, on whose bankes are rais'd a solitary yet pleasant walke where the learned Mr Hobbs invented his poeme De Mirabilibus Pecci.

Leaving this place wee came this night to lodge at Chesterfield an indifferent good towne in whose church wee saw the tombs of the Fulgiums a family once noted for an ample patrimony in these parts. The day following being Thursday the 23d Instant wee rode to Bolesover a seate of the Duke of New-Castles (being in Scarsdale) in the lower building was a spatious apartment of lofty roomes flowr'd with plaister of paris, but left unfinisht. Adjoining to it was the Managerie, and a faire stable with stone mangers, and a flat pavement. Above this stood a tower built all on arch't worke with many commodious litle roomes and chimny-peeces of marble jetting out like canopyes. The court belonging to it was inviron'd with a terra's in the manner of an amphitheater. On the same day wee went to see Hardwyck another seate appertaining to the Earle of Devonshire which came by matching into a family of the same name with the house. It is divided into two distinct buildings somwhat distant one from another; the newest whereof is well-built leaded, and batlemented round about. A large gallery, and dining roome with many antique pictures of the royall families of England; to witt the picture of the illustrious Queene Elizabeth at full length; King James when he was a lad about tenn years of age. Another of the Lady Arabella Steward in a morning-dress with long red-haire ti'd back. And in one of the roomes the figure of a large stagg made for a chimney-peece with a latine distich underneath (in letters of gold) of this ladies composing being an encomium on the stately beast. In the old building was nothing to bee seene but the library of the family wherein hung the picture of the famous Mr Hobbs in a musing posture writing his *Leviathan*. Here were great store of books but our time was too short to make any search therein. The parke here is well wooded and much better ground than that at Chatsworth. Wee retourn'd and lodg'd againe at Chesterfield this night.

On Fryday the 24th wee went as it were in a manner back againe and came to Haddon-Hall an old irregular castle-building standing upon a rock having a very steepe and ill ascent. It is now belonging to the Earle of Rutland, and descended to them by matching into the family of the Vernons; the roomes generally low, and obscure, a reverend old chappel with some Catholick remainders, at the entrance to it wee saw the tombstone of one Titus Ostitius a Legionary commander of the Romans as they tell you; but the letters were in effect totally worne out. It had formerly been dugg up out of the grounds belonging to this place. The parke and the lands here are esteemed so good, that by report the old Countess of Shrewsbury proffer'd as many shillings for one of the meadows as would surround it. Along by it runs a small river cal'd the Wyes.[174] From hence by the evening wee had mounted the tops of very lofty hills; from whose brow wee look'd downe upon severall villages in a fruitfull borne; and descending the hill wee took up our lodging at one of them nam'd Castleton which lies directly under that part of the hill where the Devils Arse is. In the morning we wrode up to the mouth of the cave, where wee alighted, and enter'd. Wee were first encountred by a regiment of ill-favor'd jades, like Gypsies, or Sybills who were very officious with their candles to conduct us;

174   Derbyshire River Wye.

these poore creatures shelter in the mouth of the cave, and dwell here in small hutts, or cottages running along in the manner of a litle village; having the conveniency of litle bartons, or backsides behind (inclos'd with loose stone) in which their carts, ricks of hay, and corn are contained. It continues with this sort of building (and withall a very lofty arch) by which meanes a glimmering light is intromitted) for the space of half a furlong or more from the entrance; but then both heigth, and light decline, so that in a short time wee were forc't to goe stooping with our candles; yet by the help of our hag like guides and the tallow-tapers, wee went on till wee came to a small current of water, where finding the passage to grow narrower and more incommoded with wett, and filth wee retourned to our horses againe; comming-back wee discharg'd our pistolls which made a mighty noise, ready to scare our ugly leaders out of their senses; having mounted wee rode up to the top of the hill where stood a sad totter'd castle (which in probability might give the name of Castleton to the village below) some would have it to bee a Roman-structure; but wee could find litle reason for that, it being so inconsiderable and unlike their wayes of building. It seemes more likely what Mr Hobs saies of it in his poem of the Peake, who conceives it to have been a place to lodge a guard in to secure the lead-workes from robbers.

Wee now passt over rocky mountains and after 2 miles riding came to Elden-Hole in the Peake forrest. This wee perceiv'd to bee a long fissure, or cleft in the rocky bowells of the earth scarse in any part more than three yards in breadth, the aforesaide learned authour Mr Hobs resembles it to a female figure cal'd a Cunnoeides, (as he does the Devils Arse of Peake to the clunes or extended buttocks of a man) perhaps occasion'd by some earth-quake. Wee rowled severall great stones of a mighty waight into the mouth of it, and then lying prostrate on the ground, wee could heare them falling, and beating to and fro for the space of four or five minutes; which makes the vulgar conceive it has no bottom. It is said that Sir Charles Candish being minded to experiment the depth of it, let downe a condemned felon (about two hundred yards with a rope, and pully) but the unhappy wretch being drawne up againe was found uncapable of retourning an answere, so that hee expir'd within a few houres.

About a mile from this is the ebbing and flowing spring which has strange vicissitudes in this nature, and about two miles distant is the hill cal'd Maim'd Tor which continually shedds it earth and the loose stones truckle from it; and yet it seems not to abate in proportion. After four miles riding farther in Darbishire wee came to lodge at Buxton a small village, yet noted for hott-springs by which many strange cures have been perform'd. I conceive there is not much doubt to bee made, but that this place might have been as usefull as the baths in Sommersetshire, had but an expense of money render'd it as acceptable to the like resort and number of gentry; for the hott springs arise in severall grounds, and places about the towne. But there is one onely at present made fitting for the use of bathing, which is in a new-built house, or Inne belonging to the the Earle of Devonshire; (hard by it is a warm spring cal'd St Annes Well;) for experience sake wee bathed in this about an hours space, and found it of a pleasing temperament somwhat more than lukewarm; but the rocky bottom so ruggid and uneven, that it made our footsteps very uncertaine. Wee saw a thick steame ascending from it in smell much after the manner of the Bath waters.

About half a mile distant from this village is a remarkable cave cal'd Pooles Hole – so named from one Poole a robber (who as they say) us'd to shelter himself in the darke cavernes hereof after the perpetration of his rogueries. Wee walk'd from our lodging to see this place, taking a lusty Smyth for our Guide, and an old bag-piper to divert us with his musick in this dolesome, and unusuall retirement. The entrance wee found so low and so inclining upon the left side, that wee were constrained to creepe in (as it were) upon our bellies; but having overcome this difficulty wee came into a place more wide and lofty, which continu'd with a kind of winding for a long space; the bottom being all of great loose stones, our Guide ever and anon show'd us the rarities of the place, as odd shapes of things in stone, and a kind of fretworke in the rock: the Queene of Scots pillar which is commonly the ne plus ultra to the women. The bed-chamber, and kitchin too of this notorious thiefe. Having walk'd in this manner about a quarter of a mile under ground wee came to a huge heape of loose stones pil'd upon one another, and after much labour, and trouble, wee climb'd it up and so came to the end of the cave. Wee found it in most places durty and flabby, by reason of the drills, and droppings of water; so that whoever enters here cannot avoide moiling himself; but the young girles and boyes of the place have gott a custome to stand ready at the caves mouth to proffer pigins of water, and herbes (for strangers to wash in) in hopes of some small gratuity.

Wee tarried here till the next day towards the evening, and then took horse, our way lying over an untoward more through a corporate towne cal'd Stopford[175] and a litle within night came to the great unincorporated towne of Manchester so noted for the trade of baies, and stuffs. In it wee saw a faire church, and an old College with some few gown-men making an externall show of learning. Hence the next morning wee went to Midleton[176] an antient

175   Stockport?
176   Middleton.

seate belonging to Sir Ralph Ashton; on the walls of the church of this village, and in the windows thereof wee saw some old inscriptions which show that it had been in this name for allmost three hundred yeares, here wee tarried till Tuesday morning and then wrode through Manchester and so to Northwich where we saw the salt-works, and tasted of the salt-springs which wee found to bee of as strong a nature as brine; wee lodged here this night, and in the morning tended towards Wood-Cote a seate belonging to the family of the Cotes's.

Hence the next morning wee went to a towne cal'd Tongue,[177] where (in the church) wee were show'd some antient tombs one of them belonging to a Lord High-Constable of England cal'd Vernon, another to a Lord Treasuror. Wee lodg'd this night being the last of August at Bromagum a towne noted for smyths[178] the next day to Coventry, and so to Mr Clarks at Watford, where wee remained all Sunday and the day following wee passt through Northampton and so to Thingdon[179] againe by the 3d of 7br. [September]

177   Tong.
178   Birmingham.
179   Findon.

10
A JOURNEY TO LINCOLNSHIRE

A Small Journey beganne in September
Ano 1678

[Note: for map see page 126]

HAVING SPENT SOME weekes in Northamptonshire, least sloth, and laziness the contagion of cuntry-gentlemen should prevaile upon mee I determin'd to traverse some parts of the adjacent counties. With this resolution on the 3d of 7br [September] this yeare I sett forward, and after some few houres riding came by an old seate of the Lord Brudenells (sonne to the Earle of Cardigan) called Deane thence to Bulleck and Colly-Weston the seates of the 2 Trions a wealthy family descended from Dutch parents. Then hard upon the going downe of the sunne wee arrived at Stanford a towne somwhat large lying by the side of a hill and fronting towards a plentifull valley. It was antiently a University; but time has allmost raz'd out all footsteps thereof except a poore ruine which they say was Brazen-Nose College.

In St Maryes church wee saw the tombe of the Lord Treasuror Burchly and descended into the vault where many of the family lay wrapt up in lead, and stone coffins. This Treasuror was the founder of Burchly House a noble old seate erected Ano. 1595 lying within 2 litle miles of this towne. As to the case of building in many respects it is litle inferior to any in England; but the inside is not so exquisite, unless antiquity may bee pleaded for it. The arches often presented to us the motto of the family *unum cor et una via*; but this want of heigth did somwhat hinder the prospect from the park, which the present possessor the Earle of Excester was reforming. Having fully view'd the house wee mounted and rode to Dunnington the first towne wee came to in the fenns of Lincolnshire. Here wee first observ'd the influence of a low flatt cuntry, most of the people throughout these parts were visited with an aguish distemper which prooved verry mortall, the inhabitants for the most part imputed to the dryness of the season; no raine falling to moysten, and coole the earth, for at least 6 months space. After this wee passed by Swineshead Abby where the men of religion called monks poysoned their Soveraign King John, so by the approach of the evening wee came to the seafaring towne of Boston.

This port is scituate in Holland beeing a low part of the cuntry having a winding channel narrow but yet deepe, and dayly attended by the tide. I know [not?] what the women may bee but else I conceive the church the fairest object in this place for voyagers, beeing a very haughty structure, and the tower perhaps as eminent in heigth as any in the nation; having been used as a pharos to guide the distressed vessels safe to the coast, the windows and loope-holes at the top were antiently sett with transparent horn, and in the midst were certaine torches plac'd in sockets, whose light beeing seene at a long distance gave greate hopes, and comfort to poore afflicted mariners. Litle else of publick note here but a place wherein they keepe their annuall mart or faire and a small Free School.

Wee went hence somwhat late in the morning and went through Kirton a noted village for pipins, after this wee forded through 2 broade arms of the sea by the help of Guides which could not have been effected otherwise without the hazard of our lives. Wee saw much sampire growing hereabouts and about 4 of the clock in the afternoone wee ferried the harbour and were sett downe at Lynne the prime port in Suffolk. It extends itself a long way upon the banke of a wide channel but somwhat choaqu'd with sand; close, and compact in building, and well stor'd with trade, having convenient places for the landing of goods. The principall things here is the old Towne-Hall and St Maryes church. Wee departed hence the next day and travelled through the fenny cuntry to Wisbidge[180] where is an old episcopall seate appertaining to Ely and some small trade by reason of a cutt made into the hart of the towne; leaving this place wee wrode along on a banke of this cutt for 5 or 6 miles and so to the episcopall see of Peterbourgh; the next day to Fotheringay to see the ruines of a noted church, in which Queene Elizabeth had erected 2 monuments in memory of 2 famous Plantagenets Dukes of York; one whereof was slaine in the Batle of Wakefield; much painting in the windows; and the falcon the devise of the House of Yorke frequently to bee seene; and by night to Thingdon.[181]

180   Wisbech.
181   Findon.

POSTSCRIPT

A VISIT TO ELTHAM

Anno 1682

O N THE 12TH of August wee went to Eltham where wee found the ruines of the antient castle belonging to the Royall Plantagenets litle now remaining but a lofty wide hall converted to a barn. The Honor of Eltham is at this time belonging to Sir John Shaw who has built a faire house upon it but verry ill seated. Here wee look'd upon the old seate of the family of the Ropers something remarkable for antiquity. On the 13th wee lay in Finsbury[182] parish and the next day went to see the ruines of Cooling castle, belonging to the famous Sir John Old-castle; who by the malice of the fraudulent clergy was executed in the raigne of Henry 5th. Greate part of the walls, and the cases of the towers yet standing with a deepe trench about it. Over the gate at the entrance is the picture of a small man in armor, with an antient character over it, and to us illegible; after this wee went to the parish of Cliff[183] to look upon an old decayed church. In the afternoone wee steered to Cobham Hall, an ample old building, lying in a wide parke belonging to the unfortunate Lord Cobham who stood attainted for treason in beginning of King James for beeing of the conspiracy with Sir Walter Raleigh, the king bestowing the forfeiture upon the then Duke of Lennox. The next day wee went to take a view of the shipps lying along the river Medway and went on board 2 of the principle viz: Brittannia the biggest first rate and of the newbuilt shipps, and next the Prince a 2nd rate of the old. The next day wee hired a smack and sailed downe to see the fort at Sheereness[184] lying upon the upmost point of the Isle of Shippy[185] opening towards the ocean inclining to the northeast. A faire gate at the entrance edg'd with stone; but the rest of the building inconsiderable; the Works on which the gunns were mounted unfinisht and the piling on the outside on the beech

182   Frindsbury.
183   Cliffe.
184   Sheerness.
185   Isle of Sheppey.

verry deficient. Good store of iron gunns planted on unstable batteries; but the sea upon violent northeast winds ready to rowle over them. In fine it is a verry unwholesome place affording no sort of accommodation either for fuell, or provision. It has taken up great store of expense, but hardly answering expectation; the chief towns on the Isle are Minster, and Quinburrow.[186]

APPENDIX

TRANSLATIONS FROM LATIN

page 14
Ædibus his ortus Mundum decoravit Erasmus
      Artibus Ingenio, Religione Fide
Fatalis Series nobis invidit Erasmum
      Sed Desiderium tollere non potuit

Raised in this house Erasmus adorned the world
With the arts through his genius and religion through his faith.
Death's course begrudged us of Erasmus
But could not take away our sense of loss [desiderius, Erasmus's name]

page 17
Accipe posteritas tua quod per sæcula narres
Taurinis Cutibus fundo solidata Columna est

Hear this so that your descendants may tell it through the generations
This column rests firmly on foundations of the hides of bulls

page 28
Haec Libertatis Ergo.

This for the sake of freedom [the civic motto of Leiden]

Presentam monstrat quolibet Herba Deum

Wherever it may be, a plant demonstrates the divine presence

page 34
virtus sola invicta

Virtue alone is invincible

186   Queenborough.

labilis hora fugit

The fleeting hour takes flight

page 35
Moribus ornata jacet hic Bona Burta Rosata

Here according to custom lies the good Bertha [of Lindsey, according to RCHM], adorned with roses.

page 42
Jesu nascenti virginiq. Matri

To Jesus, new-born, and to the Virgin Mary

page 44
Quisquis hæc legis, ita legito uti optimo principi precaberis exercitum fortem, populum fidelem, imperium securum et annos de nostris. B. B. F.

Reader, whoever you may be, so read this that for the best of princes you will pray for a strong army, a loyal populace, authority without concern, and old age, from us B B F

page 61
Ut Rosa flos florum sic est Domus istæ Domorum

As the rose is the flower of flowers, so this is the house of houses

page 62
Restitutio Regis est Solamen Gregis

The restoration of the monarch is the solace of his flock

page 67
Hac Domibus odit, amat, punit, conservat, honorat
Justitiam, pacem, crimina, jura, probos.

In these halls one hates, one loves, one punishes, one preserves, and one honours Justice, peace, accusations, judgements and proofs

page 72
Nos hæc novimus esse nihil

We know that this is nothing

page 86
Finis Damnationis Maria et origo salutis

Mary, the end of condemnation and the beginning of salvation

Page 87
Ave Filia Dei Patris
Ave Filis Dei Mater
Ave Sponsa Spiritus Sancti
Ave Totius Trinitatis Templum

Hail, daughter of God the Father
Hail, mother of god the Son
Hail, bride of the Holy Spirit
Hail, temple of the whole Trinity

page 91
Videant Senatores ne quid detrimenti Respublica capiat

Let the Senators be watchful lest the Republic should suffer any harm

Page 94
Virgo tuare fidem, virgo defende fideles
Monspelium virgo sit tibi palladium

O virgin, defend the faith, virgin protect the faithful
Virgin may you be to Montpelier their Pallas [protecting deity]

Page 98
Quo Jussa Tonantis

By which the commands of the thunderer

page 100
Divis Manibus

To the spirits of the departed

Procul este prophani

May those who are profane be far away

Trabs huius Mundi impedit volare ad Beatitudinem

This world's roof-beam prevents the flight to blessedness

page 105
Justo Dei judicio accusatus sum
Justo Dei judicio judicatus sum

Justo Dei judicio condemnatus sum

By the righteous judgement of God I have been accused
By the righteous judgement of God I have been judged
By the righteous judgement of God I have been condemned

page 106
Laetum Evangelisium

The joyful good tidings

page 107
et Anglis Regem restituit

And restored the king of England

Hoc amo quod possum qualibet ire via

This I love, that I can go wherever I choose

Page 111
O: virgo scandens, sis Marshallo cælica pandens

O virgin ascending, from heaven may you be reaching out for Marshall

Page 113
petra dic sic, quod Anselmus Episcopus est hic

You stones proclaim this, that Anselm is the bishop here

Hic jacet Medicus cujus Ruina, monstrat quod Morti, non obsistit Medicina

A physician lies here whose downfall, as his death reveals, no physic could resist

page 117
O Sancte Winifrede virgo, et Martyr ora pro nobis

O holy Winifred, virgin and martyr, pray for us

page 118
Invictæ fidelitatis præmium

The reward for unvanquished faithfulness

BIBLIOGRAPHY

SHC   Somerset Heritage Centre (SHC)
         John Walker's Commonplace Book DD/WHb/60
         Other archives:
                 DD/WHb/66
                 DD/WHb/70
                 DD/WHb/74
                 DD/WHb/136
                 DD/WHb/147

TNA   The National Archives PROB-11-476-112.pdf

ACAD   A Cambridge Alumni database
BHO   British History on line
         VCH [*Victoria County History*] *(county, vol)*
         Foster, *Alumni Oxoniensis 1500-1714*
HOP   *History of Parliament*
         Parliamentary Archives GB-061/ECU
NLS   The National Library of Scotland georeferenced first Ordnance
         Survey 1 inch maps
ODNB   Oxford Dictionary of National Biography

Wikipedia, together with the NLS maps, has been used a great deal to verify
         place-names.

Roland Allen, *The Notebook A History of Thinking on Paper* (2023)
Thomas Baskerville: *Journeys in Industrious England* ed. Anthea Jones (2023)
Jeremy Black, T*he Grand Tour in the Eighteenth Century* (1992 reprinted
         Sandpiper Books 1999)
William Camden's Britannia, a topographical and historical survey of England
         county by county (1610)

Celia Fiennes, *The Illustrated Journeys of Celia Fiennes* ed Christopher Morris
        (1982)
*The Observant Traveller Diaries of Travel in England, Wales and Scotland in
        the County Record Offices of England and Wales* ed Robin Gard
        (HMSO, 1989)
Lewis's *Topographical Dictionary* (1830)
Esther Moir, *The Discovery of Britain, the English Tourists 1540-1840* (1964)
Schellink, William, *The journal of William Schellink's travels in England 1661-
        1663*, translated from the Dutch and edited by Maurice Exwood
        and H L Lehman (Camden fifth series vol 1, 1993).
John Taylor, *Travels and Travelling 1616-1653* ed J Chandler (enlarged
        edition, Hobnob Press 2020)
*The National Gazetteer of Great Britain and Ireland (*1868)
Anthony á Wood, ed. Philip Bliss 1813-20, *Athenae Oxoniensis 3*

INDEX

For the convenience of readers, place names and relevant river and chateau names in the Low Countries and in France, referred to by Walker, are grouped together in the index, but significant people like the Prince of Orange or the Kings of France are listed in the main index.